BERLITZ®

MOSCOW
and Leningrad

1989/1990 Edition

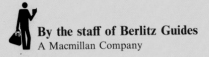

By the staff of Berlitz Guides
A Macmillan Company

Berlitz Trademark Reg. U.S. Patent Office
and other countries – Marca Registrada
Library of Congress Catalog Card No. 84-72930.

Printed in Switzerland by Weber S.A., Bienne.

6th Printing
1989/1990 Edition

How to use our guide

- All the practical information, hints and tips that you will need before and during the trip start on page 94.

- For general background, see the sections Moscow and Leningrad, p. 6, and A Brief History, p. 12.

- All the sights to see are listed between pages 19 and 74. Our own choice of sights most highly recommended is pinpointed by the Berlitz traveller symbol.

- Shopping, entertainment, nightlife and other leisure activities are described between pages 74 and 84, while information on restaurants and cuisine is to be found on pages 85 to 93.

- Finally, there is an index at the back of the book, pp. 126–128.

Although we make every effort to ensure the accuracy of all the information in this book, changes occur incessantly. We cannot therefore take responsibility for facts, prices, addresses and circumstances in general that are constantly subject to alteration. Our guides are updated on a regular basis as we reprint, and we are always grateful to readers who let us know of any errors, changes or serious omissions they come across.

Text: Ken Bernstein
Photography: cover picture, Intourist; pp. 2–3, 23, 24, 25, 27, 37, 41, 45, 56, Novosti; p. 13, Lauros-Giraudon; pp. 8, 19, 29, 33, 40, 44, Hans Keusen; p. 39, Elliott Erwitt—Magnum; pp. 46, 51, 82, 89, R. Rowan—Magnum; p. 53, John Tailor; pp. 54, 85, Emil Schulthess—Black Star; p. 75, J.N. Reichel—Réalités; pp. 17, 43, KEY-color/S. Wittwer; pp. 7, 11, 59, 60, 63, 64, 68, 71, 73, 76, 81, 83, 84, 88, 91, Daniel Vittet.
Layout: Doris Haldemann
We're particularly grateful to Simon Markis for his help in the preparation of this book. We also wish to thank Intourist, the Soviet travel bureau, for its invaluable assistance and for the cover picture.

Contents

Moscow and Leningrad

This tale of two cities contrasts Moscow, with its legendary onion-domed skyline, and the more "European" former capital, Leningrad, about 700 kilometres to the north-west. For Moscow and Leningrad are as different as Ivan the Terrible and Catherine the Great. Yet both cities share a communist way of life that jolts the visitor arriving from the West. You may not always feel at home, but with preconceptions set aside, you can combine a cultural feast with a revealing glimpse of another social system.

Moscow begins with the Kremlin, the city's geographical and historical heart. Even if nothing beyond the wall merited a glance, these 60 acres of art and architecture would still qualify Moscow as an imperative tourist attraction. Happily, the outer city fairly overflows with additional museums and galleries, music and spectacles, sights to remember. It's also the political, industrial and scientific centre of a superpower.

For all the superlatives the Soviet Union can claim as the world's biggest country, Moscow itself must affect a touch of modesty. Compared with other European capitals it's an upstart—not much more than 800 years old. By official policy its population was to have been held below 7 million through control of internal migration. But to the surprise of even the Soviet census takers,

the figure has now reached over 8 million—about the same number of people as London or New York. But its area—342 square miles—is only about half that of London.

Leningrad is the youngest and least publicized of the world's most beautiful cities. Only your own eyes can digest this feast: palaces too big to explore, painted avocado green or sky blue; a regal plaza

Unmistakably Leningrad: northern sun setting over the River Neva.

fit for the grandest parade; church spires, domes and cupolas; a park filled with classical statues, behind wrought-iron railings famous for their grace; a boulevard so urbane it does without the greenery. Here are heroic monuments to the czars, meticulously preserved by the proletarian revolution, peeling yellow houses that were home to the Pushkins and Tchaikovskys and hundreds of bridges stitching the city together across canals, tributaries and a glowering river.

By any logic these haughty charms belong somewhere far away. Yet here in what was

Card-playing or bird-watching, anyone? Candid camera catches two cheerful citizens of Moscow at a pause in their leisure activities.

a bleak northern swamp, a mighty czar ordered the construction of an imperial capital, St. Petersburg. Thousands died creating his city, hundreds of thousands more defending it.

Moscow's climate, ominously, may be described as "moderately continental". If you're an optimist, reflect that Moscow is actually only about as far north as Edinburgh. Pessimists will check the latitude of Dawson Creek, British Columbia, and Wrangell, Alaska. And Leningrad is quite simply two-thirds of the way to the North Pole. In December, beset by wet snow and Baltic gales, the number of hours of sunshine per day averages an appalling zero.

Fortunately, Russians find winter invigorating. They defy snow and cold with central heating, double windows, fur hats and frequent shots of vodka. They are great cross-country skiers, and they think nothing at all of queueing up in the snow to buy an ice-cream cone.

(In the strict sense of the word, *Russian* means a native of what's today called the Russian Soviet Federal Socialist Republic. With over three-quarters of the USSR within its borders, this republic covers roughly the original empire of Peter the Great. Today's Soviet Union claims a dozen additional republics stretching from the Baltic to the Pacific.)

Most Muscovites and Leningraders are Russian by nationality. Yet the streets of Moscow swarm with swarthy southerners, blue-eyed northerners and slight orientals—all Soviets, a sampling of more than a hundred racial groups that together make up the nation's ethnic mosaic. Like you, they're probably tourists or transients. For Moscow is where everything's happening. It's the nerve centre of all power—headquarters of the party, the government, state committees plus thousands of cultural, social and economic entities influencing the whole country.

Every Baku oilman, Irkutsk fur trapper or Pinsk librarian dreams of a trip to Moscow for business consultations, seminars or whatever other likely reason. If he can't swing it on an expense account, then he'll manage it on holiday. More than one and a half million people arrive here **9** daily by rail and air, jamming the stores (better supplied than in any other Soviet city), the cafés and sometimes the traffic.

Leningrad (population 5 million) is resigned to second place in political and industrial terms. But culturally it refuses to accept a provincial role. After all, the Hermitage remains one of the most important museums in the world. Russia's greatest authors and composers found inspiration on the banks of the Neva. Today's Leningraders consider themselves heirs to all this. They adopt a condescending attitude towards the capital, viewing it as little more than a colony of bureaucrats and transplanted peasants.

This rivalry between Leningrad and Moscow brings up some intriguing questions. Are the people of Leningrad, like the architecture, really more Western European, less Russian? Are they more sophisticated and amusing, as they claim? Do they really prefer being remote from the pressures of power?

Muscovites merely wonder whether Leningraders suffer from a superiority complex. While Muscovites share the general admiration for Leningrad's heritage, they consider the city on the Neva with its restored palaces and aura of times past as more of a museum than a metropolis. Peter the Great wanted his city to be a "window on the West", but nowadays Western ideas and fads—and problems—tend to arrive first in Moscow, where the foreign diplomats and businessmen are concentrated.

In both cities you will be intrigued by the peculiarities of Soviet life: the exhortations to the workers to fulfill the five-year production plan; the ponderous housing projects; the queues; the freshly washed streets and lavish underground stations; the coddled, swaddled children, pampered and privileged in the classless society.

Despite these contemporary similarities, no one could confuse Moscow and Leningrad... or forget them.

10

The siege of Leningrad is history now: the city survived but it has not forgotten.

A Brief History

The village of Moscow first rated mention in 1147 when it was barely a bivouac. A prince with the picturesque name of Yuri Dolgoruky—"Long-Armed George"—established the settlement on a bluff overlooking the Moskva and Neglinnaya rivers. The Kremlin's Borovitsky Gate marks the spot today. As for the rivers, the Moskva has been corseted in granite and the Neglinnaya was funneled underground more than a century ago.

As the cities of the era stacked up, Moscow was an Ivan-come-lately. But the region was hardly virgin. For centuries the river routes and thick pine forests had fairly seethed with Goths, Huns and Slavs, among other tribes. By the time Moscow was really worth pillaging, the Tartars made their first appearance. In the early 13th century these bloodthirsty but disciplined legions which had been raised by Genghis Khan surged westwards out of Mongolia, bent on conquering the world. They trampled and burned Moscow into submission.

The Muscovite princes decided that collaboration with the enemy was more profitable than resistance. Their shameless capitulation assured Moscow's success at the expense of rival Russian power centres. Chief collaborator was one Grand Prince Ivan whom the locals nicknamed Kalita, or Moneybags. The Mongols awarded him a percentage of the take to go with his more august official title of General Tax Collector.

Ivan Moneybags was shrewd enough to entice the metropolitan* of the Russian Orthodox Church to set up a see in Moscow, thenceforth Russia's ecclesiastical as well as economic and political capital. Traders, artisans and noblemen flocked to the presumably blessed city to enjoy the added protection of the newly expanded Kremlin wall.

When Constantinople fell to the Turks in 1453 Moscow became the seat of the Byzantine Church in Europe. The belief grew that Moscow was the "third Rome", the vital centre of true faith and the centre of empire.

*An Eastern Orthodox title ranking above a bishop.

Terrible Ivan

In the 16th century the city began to sprawl like a bustling metropolis around the brick walls and towers of today's Kremlin. Defences ringed defences, establishing the circular urban scheme of today. Meanwhile, in and around the Kremlin, Russia's greatest architectural masterpieces were being created. The man who

Holy Russia kept the faith when the Turks took Eastern Europe.

inspired all this dynamism was one of history's thunderbolts, Ivan IV, better known as Ivan the Terrible.

Awesome Ivan reigned for 51 years. Not everything he did was terrible. He introduced a Russian code of laws **13** and Moscow's first printing press, encouraged artists and artisans and, by his victory over the Tartars at Kazan, extended his territory to the Caspian Sea.

But he's more often remembered for other innovations. He founded Russia's first secret police. Public torture and execution became commonplace in Moscow.

Personal tragedy overtook the czar in 1581. In a fit of temper he killed his own son. After three years of haunting remorse, Ivan himself died, apparently of natural causes. By the standards of the times, this was an unusual way to go.

Ivan's heir was, unfortunately, a halfwit. The real power behind the throne, an opportunist named Boris Godunov, soon took overt control. What happened next is customarily referred to as the Time of Troubles.

In the blackest period of the Troubles, Polish forces, invited by scheming Russian noblemen, occupied Moscow. The Kremlin and a considerable part of the city were sacked. After two years of occupation, Russian popular forces rose and liberated the capital.

The Romanov Dynasty

Then a national assembly was convened to elect a new czar. The reluctant nominee was a teenager of noble birth and patriotic connections. Michael Romanov's dynasty was to rule Russia for the remaining three centuries of the empire.

Of all 18 Romanov emperors, none had greater impact on Moscow than the unpredictable autocrat, Peter the Great. For better or worse, he lived up to his title. The first czar to visit western Europe in peace, he brought back technical experts and progressive ideas. Peter the Great outlawed the oriental kowtow in his court and personally snipped off beards. He industrialized primitive factories, organized the civil service, authorized Russia's first newspaper and university, created a navy and reformed the currency, calendar and alphabet.

But behind the reformer's façade there always lurked the traditional ruthlessness. On one occasion Peter personally pronounced sentence on almost 200 men who had been obstructing his plans for westernization. Their bodies were left swinging from the Kremlin walls for months, publicizing the price of disloyalty.

Peter had brought Russia into the European diplomatic system. When he died in 1725 his permanent monument, constructed at a dreadful cost in lives and riches, was St. Petersburg, the new capital he founded facing west.

Peter the Great's Capital
Twenty thousand workmen, not exactly volunteers, began the visionary project virtually with bare hands. By thousands, they dropped from exhaustion or disease, famine or disaster. The foundations of the city, it was said, were the very bones of its builders.

Work began where Peter had turned over the first symbolic earth—on Hare Island, dominating the Neva, the obvious strategic bastion. But St. Petersburg was to be more than just a military outpost. Peter wanted a great port and metropolis. He invited foreign architects to tackle the grandiose challenge. Forty thousand more men were recruited to realize the project. So much construction material was needed that erecting stone buildings anywhere else in Russia was forbidden.

In 1712, Peter proclaimed St. Petersburg his capital. To emphasize the break with Moscow and past traditions, he commissioned a radically un-Russian cathedral on Hare Island. Instead of the cupolas of traditional Orthodox churches, it was to be a simple building with an outsized tapering spire. Peter's church was to scrape the sky, to be the highest, most pious structure in Russia.

Catherine the Great
Thirty-seven years after Peter's death began the reign of the grandest empress of them all, Catherine the Great. Catherine's prodigious love life, which she pursued into her dotage, often overshadows her other claims to fame. But history respects her talents as an empire builder. During her reign (1762–96), Russia's frontiers expanded dramatically, and the population reached 36 million, the largest in Europe. While the abuses of serfdom and autocracy became worse and worse, Catherine imported foreign artists and architects to make St. Petersburg a major capital. Tourists may overlook her many peccadilloes in view of **15**

her magnificent gift, the Hermitage. She founded the museum and sent out a network of talent scouts to buy up Europe's greatest art works.

Catherine's funny-faced son Paul reigned for only five years after her death. Some of his strange innovations set Russian civilization back appreciably. When a large, rowdy band of conspirators invaded his palace in 1801 and clumsily assassinated him, the populace was overjoyed.

Reform and Revolution

One of those implicated in the murder of Paul seems to have been his son, who inherited the throne as Alexander I. His twinges of guilt were compounded by the upbringing of an English nanny; Alexander was determined to try harder. He reversed most of his father's repressive laws and actually became a great international hero, the handsome czar who defeated Napoleon in 1812.

The 600,000-man French offensive scarcely impressed the average Russian until Napoleon entered Moscow. Then 1812 became the "Fatherland War", a patriotic agony worth fighting to the finish. Moscow itself had been abandoned to the invaders for tactical reasons. After five weeks of shivering in a ghost town, the French limped out of the Kremlin through the snow. Inspired to revenge, the Russian armies harried them to tatters all the way.

Czar Nicholas I, who took power in 1825, put down Russia's first revolution. Rebel soldiers led by reformist officers staged an uprising in St. Petersburg's Senate Square on a bitter winter day. Their revolutionary demands included the abolition of serfdom and the institution of a constitutional monarchy. The czar turned his cannon on the so-called Decembrists, killing dozens of them. After six months of interrogation, the five aristocratic ringleaders were hanged in the Peter and Paul Fortress, becoming martyrs to subsequent generations of rebel Russians. The square is now called the Square of the Decembrists in their memory.

The revolution of 1905—the first of three occurring in 20th-

On into the night, pilgrims stand in solemn tribute at Lenin's Tomb.

16

century Russia—forced concessions from the czar. Nevertheless, the violence continued on a barbaric scale on both sides. Thousands of officials were assassinated and hundreds of terrorists executed.

Petrograd

When Russia joined the Allies in World War I, superpatriots changed the name of the capital from the German-sounding St. Petersburg to Petrograd. They were much less successful in staving off defeat under any name.

Bread shortages and general hopelessness with the war set off a rumble of strikes and riots. In February 1917, protesters, strikers and army dropouts took up arms—mostly seized from military arsenals.

Within a month, Nicholas the Second—and last—abdicated. In his railway train, side-tracked at the ancient

town of Pskov, a surprised and abandoned monarch signed away 300 years of the Romanov dynasty.

Eight months later, Petrograd was the scene of the ultimate revolution. On October 24, 1917, the Bolshevik leaders, living and working at the Smolny Institute, decided to attack. In a programme promising peace, land to the peasants and power to the workers, Vladimir Ilyich Lenin and his comrades began to mould the world's first communist state.

Leningrad and Moscow

One of the early decrees stripped Petrograd of its two-century mantle of power. The new Soviet government moved to Moscow in March 1918. As Peter the Great had turned his back on the past, so Lenin abandoned the scene of czarism's heyday.

(Petrograd was renamed Leningrad after the death of Lenin in 1924.)

Lenin's successor, Joseph Stalin, inaugurated a crash programme of industrialization and collectivization of agriculture. All this ended abruptly on June 22, 1941, when Adolf Hitler's panzer divisions struck against the Soviet Union.

The two cities were subsequently proclaimed "Hero Cities". The situation in Moscow, threatened by 75 German divisions, was considered so dangerous that Soviet government officials, children and art masterpieces were evacuated. But in Leningrad the suffering was more tangible. Besieged for 900 days, a million people perished—from bombs and bullets, but mostly from starvation. Both Leningrad and Moscow held fast.

In the postwar years the Kremlin's central planners decreed great industrial expansion in both cities, along with efforts to provide housing, schools, transportation and other services. The repressive atmosphere of concentration camps inaugurated in the 1930s by Stalin was finally eased after his death in 1953. Subsequent administrations turned to the challenge of upgrading the standard of living of the Soviet people.

Today's tourists can find profound revelations in the lavishly restored legacies of the Russian past—as well as the panorama of contemporary Soviet achievement.

Moscow

Sixteenth-century town planners mapped out Moscow like a target, the Kremlin as the bull's-eye.

The innermost ring, the Kremlin wall, remains impressively intact. The second wall—protecting the area in the circumference across Red Square—lost its military significance centuries ago though relics remain. Further from the core, a third band of fortifications was built at the end of the 16th century. This was replaced by what's known simply as бульвар, the Boulevard, one of Moscow's most gracious old streets with a park in its centre. Beyond this, a nine-mile earthwork defence delineated the final city boundary. That circle is now the Garden Ring Road, a mighty traffic artery.

The only really modern addition to the ancient spider-web plan—an outer ring road, 68 miles long—marks the

Soviet provincial tourist looks at Moscow through 8-mm. viewfinder. Except for some well-defined exceptions, visitors may film freely.

recently enlarged city limits. This last of the concentric circles, Moscow's first attempt at a superhighway, ranges through invigorating open countryside.

From the lovingly restored ancient churches of the Kremlin outward to endless suburbs, the architecture tells Moscow's story like the rings of a tree trunk. The innermost churches are Byzantine, severe. The 17th century brought new colour and intricacy. Eighteenth-century mansions, now museums or institutes, show the extravagance and grace of the age. After the destruction of 1812 the government regulated rebuilding in a city-planning move to harmonize architectural lines. The more fanciful turn-of-the-century innovations gave way in the early days of Soviet rule to renowned experiments in "constructivist" techniques. But the authorities soon forbade the originality of oversized windows, circles, spirals and cubist forms. Instead Moscow built the monumental affectations of the Stalin era, followed by drab, utilitarian housing projects. Nowadays, brighter and taller apartment buildings rise in

platoons on every horizon, racing to rehouse hundreds of thousands of Muscovites every year.

But where to start seeing it all? Even if a transit traveller had only a few hours between planes, there'd be one obligatory excursion to see a living monument of Russian history, art and political power—the Kremlin.

The Kremlin

(Кремль—*kryeml'*)

In a world cluttered with wonders, few places can be guaranteed to quicken the heart. Yet even the most hardened traveller must gape with awe as he penetrates the forbidding red brick wall of the Kremlin. In this city-within-a-city, every church and palace, throne, tower and tomb, indeed every block and brick, whispers its testimony to Russia's most glorious days—and darkest nights.

The Kremlin is more than a treasury of a people's art and history. It is, as well, the actual seat of the Soviet government, not only symbolically but operationally. Because of this, substantial parts of the citadel are off-limits to tourists. The

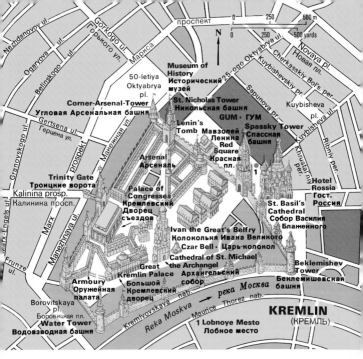

Museum of History
Исторический музей
Corner-Arsenal-Tower
Угловая Арсенальная башня
50-letiya
Oktyabrya
pl.
St. Nicholas Tower
Никольская башня
GUM · ГУМ
Spassky Tower
Спасская башня
Lenin's
Tomb Мавзолей
Ленина
Red
Square
Красная
пл.
Arsenal
Арсенал
Trinity Gate
Троицкие ворота
Kalinina prosp.
Калинина просп.
Palace of
Congresses
Кремлевский
Дворец
съездов
Hotel
Rossia
Гост.
Россия
St. Basil's
Cathedral
Собор Василия
Блаженного
Ivan the Great's Belfry
Колокольня Ивана Великого
Czar Bell · Царь-колокол
Cathedral of St. Michael
the Archangel
Архангельский
собор
Beklemishev
Tower
Беклемишевская
башня
Great
Kremlin Palace
Большой
Кремлевский
дворец
Armoury
Оружейная
палата
Borovitskaya
pl.
Боровицкая пл.
Water Tower
Водовзводная башня
Reka Moskva
река Москва
Kremlyovskaya nab.
Maurice Thorez nab.
KREMLIN
(КРЕМЛЬ)
1 Lobnoye Mesto
Лобное место

prohibited areas are easy to recognize: no-entry signs and guards will steer you away. Otherwise, you may wander at your own pace or follow a guided tour, whichever suits your mood.

Prince Yuri Dolgoruky first fenced in his domain in the mid-12th century. At intervals during the Middle Ages, invasions and disasters toppled the walls. The grand dukes of Moscow kept replacing them with ever more substantial fortifications—first of wood, then of limestone, finally brick. And with every renovation the area of the fortress seemed to expand. Three years after Colombus' voyage to America, workmen completed the red brick walls which stand today. They enclose an area **21** ten times as big as Dolgoruky's entire village.

Within the increasingly formidable defences, the elementary wooden churches and houses were supplanted by masterpieces of architecture. Local workmen built and decorated them but in most cases the czars recruited Italian architects.

In 1712 Peter the Great transplanted his capital to St. Petersburg, the northern Venice of his dreams. The Kremlin thus was demoted to the status of a ceremonial outpost, a stopover for travelling royalty and the site of pompous functions like coronations and state funerals. Twenty-five years after Peter abandoned the Kremlin, its last remaining wooden buildings were destroyed by fire. In the next major disaster, the War of 1812, luckily much of the Kremlin was saved or at least restorable.

Massive new structures were added to the ensemble in the 19th century and again in 1961 when the incongruously modern Palace of Congresses was deposited among the historic buildings. By that time the Soviet government was in residence. Huge red, electric stars balanced on the five tallest towers, and the Kremlin had been re-opened to tourists.

Each of the 20 towers along the wall has its own history and architectural eccentricities. The best known of them is the 220-foot-tall **Spassky** (Saviour) **Tower** (Спасская башня —*spasskaya bashnya*) facing Red Square. Passing through Spassky Gate, 19th-century visitors were obliged to doff their hats. In the clock tower, bells weighing up to two tons chime the quarter hours. This Russian Big Ben is heard regularly on Radio Moscow.

Only two of the towers are nameless. They guard the south wall, overlooking the river. Near the anonymous lookouts, a small five-domed cathedral was completed in 1509. The **Cathedral of St. Michael the Archangel*** (Архангельский собор—*arkhangel'skiy sobor*) combined original elements of Italian and Russian artistic traditions, opening great new pos-

---

*The Russian собор corresponds roughly to cathedral or major church of which there are many in Moscow and other Soviet cities. A cathedral, in the Russian sense of the word, isn't necessarily the seat of a bishop.

sibilities for Russian architecture. The church contains 46 tombs of princes, czars and other imperial dignitaries including the remains of Ivan the Terrible. During restoration work in the 1950s, medieval murals were discovered behind layers of dirt and dust. But the most impressive work of art found in the cathedral, a 15th-century icon of the Archangel Michael, is attributed to Andrei Rublev, the saintly genius of early Russian art.

Facing St. Michael's Cathedral across the south side of the Square of the Cathedrals, the clustering gold domes of the **Cathedral of the Annunciation** (Благовещенский собор —*blagoveshchenskiy sobor*) were built in fits and starts over the centuries. The first three cupolas date from the 15th century; six more were added in the 16th. This was the private church of the czars; the interior decorations are relatively subdued and intimate. The priceless icons are by Rublev and his celebrated teacher, Theophanes the Greek, among others. If you

Chimes of Kremlin's Spassky Tower announce the time to all Russians.

can tear your eyes away from the walls and ceilings, notice the exceptional jasper floor with its glorious colours.

The czars prayed in the Annunciation Cathedral, were buried in St. Michael's Cathedral and were crowned in the **Cathedral of the Assumption** (Успенский собор—*uspyenskiy sobor*). Crowded with works of art and traces of history, this splendidly solemn church was designed by one of the Italian architects who served the Russian throne, Aristotle Fioravanti of Bologna. One of the tragedies of the 1812 war was the way the invaders desecrated and ransacked this cathedral. By way of compensation, some of the five tons of looted silver was recaptured during Napoleon's retreat and utilized to make the main chandelier of the restored church.

Also facing the Square of the Cathedrals, the **Palace of Facets**** (Грановитая палата —*granovitaya palata*) is one of the oldest (1491) official buildings in Moscow. The Italian architects Marco Ruffo and Pietro Solario created a huge, lavish square hall with a vaulted ceiling balancing on a single, great central pillar.

*So named for the freestone of the main façade.

Czarinas and their daughters peeped down onto the gala receptions from which protocol barred them, using a grilled spy-window hidden above the carved portal.

Sightseeing in the Square of the Cathedrals, the tourist is cut off from the outer world by the ancient walls, adornments and cupolas of these memorable buildings. But all the while the eye is drawn toward the tallest structure of all. **Ivan the Great's Belfry** (колокольня "Иван Великий"— *kolokol'nya ivan velikiy*), standing like an erect telescope with an onion dome instead of an eyepiece, became the Kremlin's topmost lookout as an afterthought. The lower part was built in the early 1500s as a self-sufficient building. Nearly a century later Boris Godunov ordered escalation to a height of 263 feet that gave Moscow a 20-mile defence reconnaissance and a structure worthy of a great citadel. The biggest of 21 bells is in the shorter, adjacent tower and weighs 64 tons.

At the foot of the building

Great Kremlin Palace (below) is scene of official Soviet government receptions. Opposite: lavishly decorated portal inside the palace.

is the **Czar Bell** (Царь-коло-кол—*tsar'-kolokol*), so called because of its king-size 200-ton weight and undisputedly the world's biggest bell. A father-and-son team of Russian craftsmen, Ivan and Mikhail Motorin, cast it between 1733 and 1735. Alas, during one of the great fires a couple of years later, the great bell became red hot. When well-meaning firemen poured cold water on it, an eleven-ton chunk split off. It stands next to the rest of the delicately decorated monster.

Another prodigy of Russian foundry art, the **Czar Cannon** (Царь-пушка—*tsar'-pushka*), was never fired, either in war or peace. This ornately fili-greed triumph of psychological warfare, an antecedent of Big Bertha, dates from 1586.

Back to the architectural front. The **Patriarchal Palace** (Патриаршьи палаты—*patriarshyi palati*), the first Moscow home of the spiritual leader of the Russian church, and the adjoining **Cathedral of the 12 Apostles** (собор Двенадцати апостолов—*sobor dvenadtsati apostolov*) have been transformed into a museum. The subject is 17th-century applied art—books,

jewellery, embroidery, furniture, in all more than 700 items by Russian and foreign craftsmen in a striking setting.

The most recently opened Kremlin museum is the former **Church of the Robe of Christ** (церковь Ризположения—*tserkov' rizpolozheniya*), a small single-domed church of the late 15th century. The walls, pillars and arches of this chapel are covered with historic frescoes now restored to their original brilliance.

Unless you happen to be invited to a state reception you're unlikely to see the luxurious interior of the 19th-century **Great Kremlin Palace** (Большой Кремлевский дворец—*bol'shoy kremlyovskiy dvorets*), the yellow-and-white-walled seat of the present Soviet government. In St. George's Hall, festive champagne glasses are raised beneath six colossal bronze chandeliers glittering with 3,000 light bulbs.

But the lavish tenor of court life in imperial Russia has been meticulously preserved right next door, and it's on view to everyone. It's probably wiser to take an Intourist walk through the **Armoury** (Оружейная палата—*oru-*

zheynaya palata) to avoid the crush of ticket-buying and to have somebody to answer your questions. Under one roof has been assembled a treasure trove of art and craftsmanship. The crowns, maces, jewels and thrones of the czars compete for admiration with ancient weapons, embroidery, carvings and tapestries. Here are Ivan the Terrible's throne and crown, the silver brocade wedding gown of Catherine the Great and a hall full of imperial coaches. Don't miss one small display case of Fabergé jewellery commissioned by the imperial family showing fantasy eggs, a gold

Kremlin's Cathedral Square is crowded every day with tourists and students. The churches, with their art treasures, are now museums.

mini-train and amusing baubles of astounding workmanship. This palace, begun as imperial workshops in the 16th century, became a sort of institute of arts and crafts for the most talented Russian jewellers, icon painters, printers and leatherworkers. After the Bolshevik Revolution the exhibits were augmented by masterpieces confiscated from churches and private collectors, and the palace became a museum.

The final edifice open to the public within the Kremlin, the **Palace of Congresses** (Кремлевский Дворец съездов—*kremlyovskiy dvorets syezdov*), was constructed in little more than a year. This 1961 addition whipped up an aesthetic controversy which persists today. The designers and engineers won the Lenin Prize for their monolith of white marble and glass. Whatever your own reaction may be to its appearance and appropriateness, you'll probably be impressed once inside the building. The comfortable auditorium seats 6,000 for public concerts or private congresses of the Communist Party (whence the name Palace of Congresses).

All Palace of Congresses concert-goers must use the **Trinity Gate** (Троицкие ворота —*troitskiye vorota*) to enter and leave the Kremlin. This tallest of all 20 towers was erected in 1495. Its two-storey-deep cellars, designed as ammunition depots, also served during the 16th and 17th centuries as dungeons. This was the gate through which Napo-

leon's soldiers entered the Kremlin in September 1812. And through which, little more than a month later, they abandoned their symbolic conquest.

The Kremlin is open from 10 a.m. to 6 p.m. daily except Thursdays.

Beyond the Wall

Start your walking tour of Moscow where they stage those spectacular parades of missiles, tanks, troops, propaganda floats, workers and children bearing bouquets. Chances are your visit won't

Twenty-nine out of Moscow's 1.5 million daily visitors, these provincial tourists proudly pose for group photo on cobblestones of Red Square.

coincide with a major holiday but you won't find the place empty. As it has for centuries, **Red Square** (Красная площадь—*krasnaya ploshchad'*) tingles with life daily, though the crowds are swallowed up in its immensity. It's big enough for all the sightseers, strollers and lovers in town, with plenty of space left over. (Note that smoking is prohibited in the area.)

Once your feet have grown accustomed to the cobblestones of Red Square, you'll be impelled towards one of the best-known edifices in Christendom. For all the pictures you've seen, you still won't quite believe this architectural marvel. **St. Basil's Cathedral** (храм Василия Блаженного —*khram vasiliya blazhennovo*), with eight unmatched, weird and wonderful onion domes, proclaims its inspiration with a shout instead of a hint... and more than a slight touch of madness. It looks as if Russian architects Barma and Postnik tried and tried again to outdo one another, making one dome in the form of a pineapple, another like a tent, another a grenade—and all in unexpectedly riotous colours. One of those inevitable

legends says Ivan the Terrible brooded that an even more beautiful church might be built elsewhere for another patron. So he ordered the architects blinded (or, according to another version, beheaded).

Predictably, the 400-year-old interior of St. Basil's—now a museum—is something of an anticlimax.

On the square of St. Basil's, just in front, a circular stone structure seeming to be the pedestal for some vast vanished statue bears the name of **Lobnoye Mesto** (Лобное место). From this elevation imperial edicts were promulgated. And sometimes they were carried out on the spot whenever Czar Ivan IV chose to execute his enemies for the edification of the masses.

The low red and black modern structure alongside the Kremlin Wall, **Lenin's Tomb** (Мавзолей Ленина—*mavzoley lenina*), attracts inexhaustible queues of pilgrims. They wait for hours, in snow or sunshine, for a chance to view the embalmed body of the Soviet founder. Intourist guides

Incomparable St. Basil's Cathedral animates Red Square.

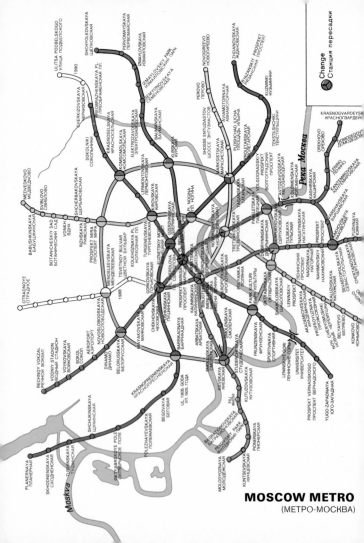

MOSCOW METRO
(МЕТРО-МОСКВА)

are authorized to escort foreigners to a spot very near the head of the line. Nearby, in the Kremlin wall itself and the adjacent garden, you can try to decipher the tombstones of heroes from Stalin to cosmonaut Yuri Gagarin, assembled in this supreme communist necropolis.

Across Red Square from the mausoleum, a far cry from all the solemnity, Russians flock to the Government Department Store, better known by its Russian acronym, **GUM** (ГУМ). From the inside, this bizarre Victorian structure resembles an overgrown greenhouse or a Jules Verne dirigible hangar. Eighty-five million customers a year jostle for food, clothing, TV sets, gadgets and souvenirs. You'll want to join the throngs for a look at the airy architecture and an insight into the standard of living.

Take a look, too, at the major shops along bustling **Gorky Street** (улица Горького—*ulitsa gor'kovo*), Moscow's liveliest thoroughfare. They specialize in, for instance, dairy products or foreign-language books, sausages or synthetic fabrics. A couple of lavishly chandeliered pre-revolutionary shops have been preserved more or less as they looked when the only patrons were aristocrats. Gorky Street is so animated that the locals jokingly call it Broadway. But the bright lights here were reserved for holidays.

Nearby Sverdlov Square (площадь Свердлова—*ploshchad' sverdlova*) was known before the revolution as Theatre Square. The world-famous **Bolshoi Theatre** (Большой театр—*bol'shoy teatr*) has been on this square since 1824. Four bronze steeds charging from the top of a monumental colonnade crown this gracious structure. The interior of red and gold is almost sinfully sumptuous. The luxury of all this and the opportunity to attend a performance of the Bolshoi opera and ballet companies make for an unforgettable experience. Intourist furnishes tickets to foreign visitors on a first-come-first-served basis. The leading artists often play out of town—the price of fame. But no matter who's on stage, you won't regret a visit to the Bolshoi.

In few cities would the underground railway system be listed among the most interesting tourist attractions, but in

Moscow the **metro** (метро) is a must. A 5-kopek coin buys you unlimited mileage on the fast, cheerful, frequent trains. But the trip is almost beside the point. It's the stations themselves which amaze the visitor: heroic sculptures, mosaics, paintings, carvings, stained-glass hymns to revolution. The newer, less central stations have economized on the artistic flourishes but they're also distinctive and spotlessly clean. Passengers are plunged from street level to platform level on express escalators. Though the actual depth of the tube is something of a military secret, you'll notice it's substantially deeper than the London underground or American subways.

If you emerge from the metro at the Arbatskaya (Арбатская–*arbatskaya*) station you can do an easy walking tour through three centuries. Some of the crooked streets around **Arbat Square** (Арбатская площадь—*arbatskaya ploshchad'*) comprise a charming memento of Old Russia, with 18th- and 19th-century houses undisturbed. The small shops merit a major window-shopping stroll. Just around the corner, by contrast, the new

Kalinin Avenue (Проспект Калинина–*prospekt kalinina*) reveals a Soviet version of the metropolis of the future. Rows of sleek 22- and 25-storey apartment and government buildings perch upon a sprawling two-storey shopping and entertainment centre. This boulevard boasts Moscow's biggest supermarket, biggest bookshop and a restaurant in which fully 2,000 diners can await service at the same time. At the far end of the long avenue, a 31-storey building in the shape of an open book tops off this showpiece experiment in urban planning. It's the headquarters of Comecon, Eastern Europe's Council of Mutual Economic Assistance, the rough equivalent of Western Europe's Common Market.

Just across the Moskva River, by the way, you can't avoid noticing the **Hotel Ukraina** (гостиница ''Украина''—*gostinitsa ukraina*), one of seven overpowering buildings erected in Moscow in the late 1940s and early '50s. With their huge needle spires and ostentatious frills, all seven look confusingly alike.

Southward along the riverside highway appears a more modest ''kremlin'' of haunting

Moscow University: biggest of seven look-alike Stalinesque skyscrapers.

beauty. Behind a crenellated wall with a dozen watch-towers, **Novodevichy Convent** (Новодевичий монастырь —*novodyevishchiy monastir'*) was founded in the early 16th century as a combined military and religious outpost. Among the sensuous onion domes, Peter the Great imprisoned his sister Sophia for presumed political infidelity. The corpses of his enemies were strung outside her window to prove he was serious. The church within the convent walls is the seat of the metropolitan, the spiritual leader of the city's Orthodox Christians. In the tranquillity of the convent cemetery, sombre monuments mark the tombs of outstanding figures from Russian history, but unfortunately tourists are not always allowed in.

On the south bank of the river, another of those ornate skyscrapers burdens the horizon. This 32-storey tower, supporting a 196-foot spire topped by a red star, houses **Moscow State University** (Московский Государственный Университет—*moskovskiy go-* **37** *sudarstvenniy universitet*) and a goldmine of statistics.

Nearly 32,000 scholars pursue 14 fields of study here in a thousand labs, 148 auditoriums and 45,000 halls, rooms, nooks and crannies. When they lift their heads from their books, the students may enjoy a splendid panoramic view over Moscow. Tourists share it from the observation deck built on the edge of the bluff. Note, too, the charming little church just to the left of the lookout point. It's one of about 50 Moscow churches where religious services are still conducted.

Luzhniki Park (Лужники—*luzhniki*), across the river, is described as Europe's biggest sports complex. More than 100 million cubic feet of earth were trucked in to raise 450 acres of meadowland above flood level. The park includes running tracks, tennis courts, a swimming pool, sports palace and **Lenin Stadium** (Центральный стадион имени Ленина—*tsentral'niy stadion imeni lenina*), seating 100,000 fans.

Closer to the heart of town, the **Moscow Swimming Pool** (Плавательный бассейн ''Москва''—*plavatyel'niy bas-seyn moskva*) is claimed to be Europe's largest. In winter the heated water sends up an eerie fog visible over much of the city. Three million year-round enthusiasts, wearing obligatory bathing caps, frolic or work out in this gigantic circular open-air pool. It was opened in 1960 where formerly Moscow's most richly decorated church stood, pulled down after the revolution. The Church of the Redeemer commemorated the capital's deliverance in 1812. After it was

Handle with care

For an outsider, the Russian name game is just too much.

Take Aleksei Ivanovich Petrov—Aleksei, son of Ivan, of the Petrov family.

If you're a stranger, call him Mr. Petrov. (Don't call him comrade unless you're a member of the Communist Party.)

If you're acquainted but don't know him well, use the title Aleksei Ivanovich—the last name omitted.

If he's your pal, call him Aleksei.

If you're very close, use a nickname. A standard diminutive of Aleksei, for instance, is Lyosha.

No wonder Russian novels are so complicated.

demolished, efforts to construct a monumental Soviet government building in its stead persistently failed, creating a rich folklore among superstitious Muscovites. At last the swimming pool was decided upon to utilize the difficult terrain.

After gawking at so many buildings and things, old and new, a closer look at the people may refresh the eyes and mind. For the fun of it, stroll through **Gorky Park** (Парк культуры и отдыха имени Горького—*park kul'turi i otdikha imeni gor'kovo*), officially called the Central Park of Culture and Leisure Named After Gorky. The 300-acre recreation ground consolidates many pre-revolutionary gardens into an amusement park with grass, trees, statues and martial music blaring from loudspeakers. See Muscovites squealing on the ferriswheel, singing, boating, devouring snacks, courting, dancing, laughing. Amid the monumental and abstract superlatives which tend to overpower tourism in the USSR, real life and real people are a reassuring breath of air.

Muscovites relax over chessboards, but champions train full time and receive heroes' treatment.

Behind eccentric façade of Tretyakov Gallery, a treasure-house of art.

Museums and Galleries

Harried and footsore, many a tourist may skip the odd cultural outing in favour of a siesta. Fair enough. But a couple of Moscow's museums are truly not to be missed.

Hours vary, but are normally from 10 or 11 a.m. to 6 or 7 p.m. All museums close one day a week, often on Mondays, and on the first or last day of the month. An entrance fee is usually charged. The most "must" museum of all is the **Tretyakov Gallery** (Третьяковская галерея —*tretyakovskaya galereya*). Don't be put off by the building itself. Those stern brick walls surround a world-famous collection of Russian art. The building and the first 1,500 paintings were willed to the city of Moscow by a 19th-century patron of the arts, Pavel Tretyakov.

Experts may argue the merits of Leningrad's Hermitage versus the Paris' Louvre or New York's Metropolitan, but in at least one field the Tretyakov wins hands down. It's the all-time treasure-house of old Russian religious art. Among the exhibits: *The Virgin of Vladimir,* an early 12th-century Byzantine icon of such sensitivity and grace that it set the standard for generations of devout Russian artists. Two rooms of the Tretyakov are crammed with these venerated glories of the nation's distant past.

Other attractions here are historical paintings on distinctive Russian themes. See the evocative *Ivan the Terrible with the Body of His Son* and *Volga Boatmen,* both by Ilya Repin, the great 19th-century realist. And join the crowds examining the enormous canvas called *The Appearance of the Messiah before the People* by Alexander Ivanov. It took him 20 years to paint.

The Tretyakov also devotes a great deal of space to recent Soviet art, including a generous helping of those triumphant riveters and fulfilled milkmaids designed to inspire the labours of the citizenry.

Next: The **Pushkin Fine Arts Museum** (Музей изобразительных искусств имени Пушкина—*muzey izobrazi-*

Tretyakov's art collection includes 15th-century icon by Andrei Rublev.

tel'nikh iskusstv imeni pushkina) with its classic white marble façade. In spite of its location across the street from the Moscow Swimming Pool, the Pushkin even *looks* the part of a great museum.

Dedicated to the history of world art, its impact reverberates in many directions, from antiquity to the 20th century. Under one roof are statues and reliefs from Babylon and Egypt, along with classical art to compete with the great collections in Europe. Here are **41** masterpieces by Botticelli, Canaletto, El Greco, Rembrandt, Rubens. And as for French artists, the Pushkin Fine Arts Museum offers a dazzlingly impressive lineup: Cézanne, Corot, Gauguin, Manet, Matisse, Monet, early Picasso, Renoir, Toulouse-Lautrec and Van Gogh...to name the top ten. Russian collectors were among the first to appreciate them.

The institution used to be known as the Alexander III Museum of Fine Arts, which may have avoided a bit of confusion. For today only a few blocks from the Pushkin Fine Arts Museum is the **Alexander Pushkin Museum** (Музей Пушкина—*muzey pushkina*). The two establishments have nothing in common except for the use of the poet's name and the classical columns adorning

Russian Writers

World literature acknowledges a major debt to the Russian writers of the 19th century. Four of the all-time greats are commemorated in their own Moscow museums:

ALEXANDER SERGEEVICH PUSHKIN (1799–1837). Every Russian schoolchild can quote, with pride and pleasure, page after page of the poetry of Pushkin. The author of the verse novel *Eugene Onegin,* the romantic verse tale *The Prisoner of the Caucasus* and the tragedy *Boris Godunov* is the undisputed national genius, credited with "inventing" the modern Russian language.

FYODOR MIKHAILOVICH DOSTOEVSKY (1821–81) stood before a czarist firing squad and lived to write about it. Czar Alexander II pardoned him at the last minute. Dostoevsky later wrote about the experience in *The Idiot. Crime and Punishment* and *The Brothers Karamazov* plumb timeless psychological depths.

LEO (LEV) NIKOLAYEVICH TOLSTOY (1828–1910), a Russian count and philosopher, wrote what may be the greatest novel ever created, *War and Peace* (1863–69), as well as the unforgettable *Anna Karenina.*

ANTON PAVLOVICH CHEKHOV (1860–1904) inspired other writers with credible characters and brooding conscience in his stories and long-lived plays—*The Seagull* (1896), *Uncle Vanya* (1900), *The Three Sisters* (1901), *The Cherry Orchard* (1901).

Moscow wedding on high, with the city as backdrop.

their structures. The Alexander Pushkin Museum (the one without "fine arts" in its title) houses manuscripts and personal possessions of the revered national poet. The building itself is interesting—a stuccoed timber classic dating back to 1814.

Other literary figures are also honoured in widely dispersed museums of varying importance. Bookworms may choose the **Chekhov** (Музей Чехова —*muzey chekhova*), **Dostoevsky** (Музей Достоевского—*muzey dostoyevskovo*), **Gorky** (Музей Горького —*muzey gor'kovo*), **Mayakovsky** (Музей Маяковского **43**

Letters imperfect

Do you think the Russian language is indecipherable? Take heart; it could have been worse.

In ancient days the Greek-based 43-letter Cyrillic alphabet was considerably more complicated. Then Peter the Great ordered major simplifications. The next big shakeup came in 1917 when the Provisional Russian Government killed off four redundant letters.

Now there are a mere 32 letters in the Russian alphabet, from а to я. Two of them—ь and ъ—have no sound at all.

—*muzey mayakovskovo*) or **Tolstoy** (Музей Толстого — *muzey tolstovo*)—or the **Literature Museum** (Литературный музей —*literaturniy*

muzey) containing manuscripts and first editions by all manner of Russian writers.

Nor are lovers of other arts neglected when it comes to studiously organized archives. The **Bakhrushin Theatrical Museum** (Театральный музей имени Бахрушина —*teatral'niy muzey imeni bakhrushina*) illustrates two centuries of drama, ballet and opera in Russia through costumes, sketches, portraits and rare playbills.

The **Glinka Museum of Musical Culture** (Музей музыкальной культуры имени Глинки—*muzey muzikal'noy kul'turi imeni glinki*) clutters an old mansion with 1,500 musical instruments plus writings and orchestrations from the pens of the great composers, Russian and foreign.

Returning to the visual arts, Moscow's **Museum of Oriental Arts** (Музей искусства народов Востока—*muzey iskusstva narodov vostoka*) is billed as the most complete in the USSR for Chinese, Japanese and Indian workmanship, as well as for handicrafts from the Soviet Far East.

The **Museum of Folk Art** (Музей народного искусства—*muzey narodnovo iskusstva*), just off Gorky Street in the heart of the downtown district, displays intricately designed Palekh boxes, wood carvings, embroidery.

The **Museum of Serf Art** (Музей творчества крепостных—*muzey tvorchestva krepostnikh*) is a monument to the gifted artists and artisans among the millions of Russians held in bondage until emancipation in 1861. This 18th-century timber palace was built and exquisitely decorated by a brigade of serfs directed by a brilliant architect-artist who was himself a serf. The **Ostankino Palace** (Останкинский дворец—*ostankinskiy dvorets*), as it's also known, is set in a pleasant park in northern Moscow.

Left: Browsing among cheap, mass-circulation books in the open air; controversial works are instant sell-outs. Below: Several Moscow museums cover achievements of Russian applied arts; this precious enamelwork from the 16th century is in Kremlin Armoury.

Back to Square One, where Moscow's oldest museum occupies a turreted red-brick building facing gloomily across several hundred yards of Red Square toward St. Basil's Cathedral. The **History Museum** (Исторический музей—*istoricheskiy muzey*) illustrates the evolution of the many peoples inhabiting today's Soviet Union. Exhibited are hundreds of thousands of individual items—ancient tools and weapons, coins, ornaments, costumes and even Napoleon's abandoned bed.

Three Moscow museums specialize in revolutionary themes:

The **Lenin Museum** (Музей Ленина—*muzey lenina*) fills more than 20 halls of a former city-council building with papers and objects illuminating the life and work of the founder of the Soviet state. A replica of Lenin's Kremlin study, exact down to the last pencil and notebook, faithfully reproduces a corner of the Council of Ministers Building, closed to all but the veriest VIPs.

The **Museum of the Revolution** (Музей Революции —*muzey revolutsii*) is housed in a distinguished three-storeyed building on Gorky Street, once the English Club, a fashionable hangout for foreigners and Russian aristocrats. Nowadays this stately colonnaded structure is devoted to documenting three critical 20th-century upheav-

Monument symbolizing blast-off hails Soviet triumph in space travel.

als in Russia: the 1905 revolution, the February revolt of 1917 and the Great October Socialist Revolution that followed.

As for the **Marx-Engels Museum** (Музей Маркса и Энгельса—*muzey marksa i engelsa*), appropriately located at 5, Marx-Engels Street, this is where to see manuscripts and personal effects of the theoreticians of communism.

No. 38, Kutuzov Avenue is the address for a museum built around a single painting. Some painting! It's about 380 feet long and 50 feet high, done by an artist named Franz Roubaud for the centenary of the 1812 war. (See page 16.) This vast recreation of the critical struggle is housed in a cylindrical building called the **Battle of Borodino Panorama Museum** (Музей-панорама "Бородинская битва"—*muzey-panorama borodinskaya bitva*).

Just behind the museum is the so-called **Kutuzov Hut** ("Кутузовская изба"—*kutuzovskaya izba*). This reconstruction marks the site where the decision to abandon Moscow was made by Field Marshal Mikhail Kutuzov, after whom the avenue is named.

In the same area is a statue of Kutuzov and an obelisk marking the common grave of 300 army casualties of the Borodino battle with the French in 1812.

In all, more than 60 Moscow institutions, large and small, are classified as museums. They always seem packed with fanatical culture-hoarders. You may not be able to maintain interest and endurance after a few days on the gallery rounds. But try to set aside half a day to visit the biggest "museum" in town— a permanent outdoor exposition with scores of pavilions set among gardens, fountains and statues. In theory, at least, it ought to have something for everyone...

ВДНХ

No one thought to devise a catchy name like Expo Moscow or Progressland. Russians never use the official name, just the initials—ВДНХ, pronounced *vay day en kha*. No wonder, since the official title is: Exhibition of Economic Achievement of the USSR.

Everything about the exhibition is grandiose, starting even before you enter. Just beside the metro station is a **47** shimmering obelisk as tall as a 30-storey building. This streamlined shaft of titanium-plated steel represents the blast-off of a spaceship. The monument's base is big enough to house a museum devoted to Soviet space super-latives.

Another oversized monument stands far to the right of the exhibition's main gate. This is the 1937 Socialist Realism statue, *Worker and Woman Collective Farmer*, a hammer-and-sickle slogan in stainless steel. It weighs 75 tons.

Once inside the ceremonial gate (admission charge gives unlimited access to all the pavilions) you'd best decide on an agenda. The place is much too big for aimless wandering.

If you're interested in agriculture, for instance, there are separate buildings on irrigation, cattle breeding, horse breeding, fur-bearing animals and Soviet agriculture in general. Actually, ВДНХ started out in 1939 as a sort of gigantic county fair, then branched into industry, science and culture.

Many tourists are impressed by the pavilion called **Cosmos**—easy to find because of the life-sized spaceship assembled outside. Vivid exhibits and mementoes inside the hangar-like structure span the history of Soviet space exploration. Full-sized models of sputniks dangle from the ceiling.

Other buildings around the fairgrounds concentrate on perhaps less glamorous aspects of technology—those vaunted Soviet hydroelectric systems or working models of blast furnaces. Country folk come to admire displays of Soviet consumer goods, extant and planned.

If your tour of the USSR will take you on to more of the 15 Soviet republics—the Ukraine or Georgia, for example—this exhibition is the place to get a preview of the regional customs, costumes and cooking.

ВДНХ is serious business, designed to impress visiting foreigners and Soviets alike with the nation's talents and strengths. It's by no means an amusement park. But thanks to snack bars, cafés, restaurants, the landscaping effort and a few sideshows, the heavy-handed message may be relieved with a bit of relaxation.

Day Trips from Moscow

For a change of pace, a drive through inviting countryside and a destination worth visiting, here are some excursions near and not-so-near to Moscow. The list is arranged by distance, the closest first. Most visitors take Intourist coach tours, offered certain days of the week according to a schedule posted at your hotel service bureau. (But ask for confirmation, as the timetable may be out-of-date.) If you're driving yourself, be sure to clear out-of-town trips in advance with Intourist. The highway patrol takes the formalities seriously;

One Day Trips

KLIN
КЛИН

Dmitrov
Дмитров

ZAGORSK
ЗАГОРСК

Aleksandrov
Александров

Solnechnogorsk
Солнечногорск

ABRAMTSEVO
АБРАМЦЕВО

Fryanovo
Фряново

Volokalamsk
Волоколамск

Sheremetyevo
Шереметьево

Khimki
Химки

Mitishchi
Мытищи

Noginsk
Ногинск

Istra
Истра

MOSKVA
МОСКВА

ARKHANGELSKOYE
АРХАНГЕЛЬСКОЕ

KUSKOVO
КУСКОВО

Orekhovo-Zuyevo
Орехово-Зуево

Vnukovo
Внуково

BORODINO
БОРОДИНО

Moskva
р. Москва

GORKI LENINSKIYE
ГОРКИ ЛЕНИНСКИЕ

Ramenskoye
Раменское

Podolsk
Подольск

Naro-Fominsk
Наро-Фоминск

Domodedovo
Домодедово

Moskva
р. Москва

Voskresensk
Воскресенск

Chekhov
Чехов

Nara
р. Нара

Obninsk
Обнинск

Kolomna
Коломна

Oka
р. Ока

Serpukhov
Серпухов

Oka
р. Ока

MOSKVA AND VICINITY
(МОСКВА И ЕЕ ОКРЕСТНОСТИ)

N

if you haven't filed a "flight plan" you risk being sent back to Moscow.

First, an in-town excursion, so near that you can go by metro: Zhdanovskaya (Ждановская) line to Ryazansky Avenue (Рязанский проспект —*ryazanskiy prospekt*) station. **Kuskovo** (Кусково) was the estate of Prince Peter Sheremetev who owned 150,000 serfs. Quite a few of them were mobilized at Kuskovo to build a stately wooden palace and a formal park to enhance it. The palace now contains a ceramics museum with displays of historic or artistically notable items.

Less than 30 kilometres from the centre of Moscow, at **Arkhangelskoye** (Архангельское), another prince's palace merits a visit. Prince Yusupov not only owned plenty of land and serfs. He was also a theatre producer and museum curator. The happy ensemble of palace and park proves his good taste. Note the works of art and appointments in the formal rooms of the great house. Elsewhere on the grounds, visit the famous 19th-century theatre, now an exhibition hall, which was run by the prince's serfs.

Gorki Leninskiye (Горки Ленинские), about 35 kilometres from central Moscow, is a village of serious significance to the Soviets. In a columned two-storey house on a former private estate, Vladimir Lenin spent the last months of his life. The house is now a memorial museum, the furnishings preserved just the way they were when he died there on January 21, 1924.

Abramtsevo (Абрамцево), an estate about 60 kilometres by road from Moscow, has interesting artistic associations. In the mid-19th century, the owner was Sergei Aksakov, a writer who fictionalized the aristocratic atmosphere in which he lived. Among his frequent guests were literary figures like Gogol and Turgenev. Later the estate was bought by a tycoon and art collector who turned it into a hangout for artists and actors. All this lively past is commemorated in the main house, now a museum. The park around it is designed for relaxation. But note the odd replica of a late 19th century church.

Onion domes of Zagorsk cathedral (opposite) brighten winter scene.

50

If you can spare a day for only one outing outside Moscow, the consensus of experts and satisfied customers alike must point to **Zagorsk** (Загорск). About a 75-kilometre drive north-east of Moscow, Zagorsk is a bonanza of ancient Russian art and architecture. It's also, to this day, a place of pilgrimage of the fervent faithful and the seat of the Russian Orthodox Church.

A monk named Sergius founded Trinity Monastery (now Trinity-St. Sergius) in the first half of the 14th century. It was a religious and military outpost of Moscow, the sort of place most likely to face the Tartar hordes. This happened repeatedly with bloody consequences. History also acclaims the monastery's 17th-century defenders who survived a 16-month siege by 15,000 Polish and Lithuanian aggressors. A final historical claim to fame: Peter the Great took refuge here when he believed his enemies were closing in. After his initial panic, the young czar was able to turn events to his favour, transforming the monastery into a temporary power base.

The most important archi-tectural achievement within the fortress walls, Holy Trinity Cathedral, dates from 1423 and is the patriarch's church. Russia's legendary icon painter, Andrei Rublev, created some of his greatest works on the walls and iconostasis* of this church. He was elevated to sainthood in the Russian Orthodox Church, as was Sergius, the monastery's founder.

By command of Ivan the Terrible, the Cathedral of the Assumption was added to the monastery complex. Its five outsized domes in blue and gold are a hymn to Russian faith and art.

In addition to the obvious attractions, this walled town also offers two museums. One documents the history of the monastery itself. The other shows off cottage craftsmanship, particularly sculpted children's wooden toys. (The area around Zagorsk has been famous for its toy production for centuries.)

Further yet from Moscow—about 90 kilometres along the highway to Lenin-

---

*The screen or partition with doors and icon panels which separates the nave from the sanctuary in Eastern Orthodox churches.

grad—a pleasant day trip leads to the 14th-century town of **Klin** (Клин). This was the home of Tchaikovsky where he found the "all-pervading quiet" he needed. The house is restored just as he had arranged it, piano and all.

Finally, an excursion into history which inspired not only Tchaikovsky but Tolstoy and packs of authors and artists who followed. **Borodino** (Бородино), about 125 kilometres west of Moscow, was the site of the most dramatic battle of the 1812 war. In 15 hours of agony, perhaps

Special ceremony in Zagorsk, patriarchal seat of Russian Orthodox Church, provides occasion for reunion of prelates from faraway cities.

100,000 soldiers were killed or wounded, and Napoleon learned that the Russians could stand and fight. Remnants of the earthworks can still be traced; dozens of monuments, Russian and French, solemnize the scene.

History's irony chose Borodino as a battlefield of a second war. In 1941–42, heavy fighting took place here between the Nazi invaders and Soviet defenders of the Moscow salient. Monuments proliferated.

Soviet troops carried battle trophies to Red Square to mark victory in World War II. Peacetime parades (below) still stress patriotism.

Moskva River Cruise

If the weather's fair, try to squeeze in a Moskva River jaunt. It's an invigorating style of rubbernecking with fresh air and the adventure of a boat trip plus a fish-eye's view of famous sights.

You can board one of the "river trams", as they're known, at the embarkation point near the Kievsky railway station (Киевский вокзал —*kiyevskiy vokzal*), where three metro lines converge. The trip ought to run less than an hour and a half. Not the least pleasant surprise is the very reasonable fares.

The first major event after anchors aweigh is the fairytale skyline of **Novodevichy Convent:** a 17th-century belfry floating above the five onion domes of a 16th-century cathedral, all behind fortress walls.

Moscow State University with its monolithic skyscraper dominates the bluffs far above on the right bank. What looks like a huge ski-jump is indeed a ski-jump for the very brave.

The boat slips beneath a novel bridge, a double-decker with a glassed-in lower level which happens to be a metro station suspended over the Moskva River.

Gorky Park, along the right bank, sprouts sky-rides above tree-level.

You'll be able to distinguish the **Crimean Bridge,** a graceful suspension bridge across the Moskva. With six lanes for motor traffic, it was built in 1938, a big year for river improvements here.

You can get your bearings from the improbable, streamlined tower on your left. It's the top of the high-diving board at the **Moscow Swimming Pool.**

The next bridge, called the **Great Stone Bridge,** is really made of steel and cast-iron. It retained the name of an ancient stone bridge which was the first arch to span the Moskva; 1938, again.

And then comes the highlight of any Moscow tour, by land or water, the **Kremlin.** With the changed perspective, you may see unexpected delights: details of the wall and its battlements, the grace of the bell tower topping the other Kremlin domes, the blinding golds and whites against the blue of a fresh sky.

The right bank of the river here is called the **Maurice**

View across the Moskva and down Kutusov Avenue, a wide-angle lens gives an insular look to this section of the Soviet capital.

Thorez Embankment in honour of the late French communist leader. The Union Jack identifies the mansion occupied by the British Embassy.

Next, on the opposite bank, you could hardly miss the **Rossia Hotel,** a modern block of Pentagonesque proportions, containing two cinemas, a concert hall, restaurants, shops and 6,000 beds.

Just after the next bridge the **Yauza River** empties into the Moskva. It's all been tidied up behind granite embankments, a far cry from the muddy scene when Peter the Great took up sailing there.

Another of those ponderous

skyscrapers coming up on the left indicates the ride is nearly at an end. Incidentally, this palatial pastry is not a ministry, a hotel or a university but a residential building.

You may want to get off the boat at the pier near Krasnokholmsky Bridge (Краснохолмский мост—*krasnokhomskiy most*), one stop *after* the apparent end of the trip when the boat begins to double back. This stop is a short walk from the Taganskaya (Таганская) metro station on the Circle Line to everywhere.

If your sea legs crave more satisfaction, and you have the time, more elaborate cruises are available. The place to embark is the Northern River Station (Северный речной порт—*severniy rechnoy port*), an unlikely bit of Soviet architecture designed like an impossible stone ship and set beside the Khimki Reservoir (Химкинское водохранилище—*khimkinskoye vodokhranilishche*) on the Moscow canal. The bustling passenger terminal is a short walk through a well-planned park from the River Station (Речной вокзал—*Rechnoi vokzal*) metro stop. Even if you don't take a cruise you may want to try for a table in the terminal's Volga Restaurant (ресторан "Волга"), well known for its fish menu and the view.

The reservoir here is part of an elaborate modern interconnection of the Moskva River with the Volga, assuring the capital of its drinking water and providing a navigational system linking the Baltic with the Black Sea.

Short and long trips originate here during the summer, on minor excursion boats, solid cruise liners and high-speed hydrofoils. Even the briefest excursion unveils a bracing horizon of wide-open northern country—pines and birches and simple hamlets, overdeveloped in spots by high-tension lines, youth camps and workers' sanitariums.

Summer is brief hereabouts so it's no wonder the multitudes crowd to Khimki for sun and scenery. By the way, those overnight cruise ships are just about the only places in the Soviet Union where sleeping accommodation is available without proof of identity. Some romantic young couples flocking aboard seem to have heard about this oversight in a society of strict social codes. **57**

Leningrad

Whatever your travel arrangements, any visit to the Soviet Union which skips Leningrad is unfinished business. Even if you can only organize a couple of days in the dream city of Peter the Great, do it. A brief look is better than none at all.

Why all the fuss? Leningrad is mist enveloping a baroque bridge. Sea wind sweeping the plaza where a revolution was won. The dark back streets of Dostoevsky and Rasputin. The hustle of the Nevsky Prospekt, or avenue. An inspired city of art, statues and parks, and good taste. And the Leningraders, indomitable folk, proud, wry.

Like Venice and Amsterdam, Leningrad crouches on water, criss-crossed by rivers and canals, sewn together by hundreds of bridges, ceremonial or quaint or humdrum. The principal waterway is the River Neva, leading eventually to the Gulf of Finland. Inside Leningrad, the Neva is contained within granite banks, but it remains so wide and dramatic that its influence on the city rarely slips from consciousness. When its long winter's ice suddenly shudders and cracks, the river rejuvenates the city. And on the "white nights" of summer, when night never really falls, the twilit sky meets the grey water and stops all time. Sometimes it's hard to believe that this is a real city inhabited by people who go to work in factories, shipyards and offices.

North of the Neva

The **Peter and Paul Fortress** (Петропавловская крепость —*petropavlovskaya krepost'*), dominating the river Neva, was Peter the Great's first project in his new city. This stronghold, controlling river navigation, was started in 1703 with walls of wood and mud, but evolved into a proper citadel, protected by impressive red-brick ramparts.

When the fortress lost most of its military significance, these formidable walls were used for other ends. Politi-

Symbol of old St. Petersburg: slender gilt spire of Peter and Paul Cathedral glints in autumn sunlight across the mighty River Neva.

cal prisoners, including many famous revolutionaries, were held in the **dungeons.** The czar's own son, Alexis, spent six months in a cell here before being tortured to death by order of his father.

The walls also protect the former royal mint, which now coins Soviet money. Warning: daily at noon a cannon goes off to officially mark the time of day.

The dominant building within the fortress walls is the **Peter and Paul Cathedral.** Of Dutch style, it was erected by Swiss architect Domenico Trezzini between 1714 and 1733, but was later renovated. The fragile spire, covered with gold leaf, supports an angel

To the greater glory of God: sumptuous decoration adorns the interior of Peter and Paul Cathedral.

bearing a cross. Peter is buried in this church, as are most of his successors.

The oldest house in town is **Peter's Cottage** (Домик Петра—*domik petra*), thrown together in 1703 for the czar's shelter—preserved to this day within a stone building serving as a museum.

Not far from here is moored the cruiser **Aurora** from which was fired the signal for the Bolshevik assault on the Winter Palace in 1917. The Aurora with her three old-fashioned funnels tall and grave, Titanic style, is now a historic monument.

South of the Neva

No square in Europe is more aristocratic than **Palace Square** (Дворцовая площадь —*dvortsovaya ploshchad'*) in Leningrad, still dominated by a monument to a czar. The Alexander Column (155 feet high) is said to be the biggest single slab of granite standing anywhere. The south side of the immense open square borders the old General Staff Headquarters of the czarist army, a classical curve with a built-in ceremonial arch.

The north side of the ex-panse is filled by the **Winter Palace** (Зимний дворец—*zimniy dvorets*). Painted a surprising green with white details, this Russian baroque building holds at least three claims to fame. First, it is historically fascinating as the home of the last six czars. Second, it houses the Hermitage Museum (see page 66). Third, it is an architectural classic. Built in the mid-1700s, the Winter Palace was the climax of Count Bartolomeo Rastrelli's quest for an architectural style unique to St. Petersburg. Rastrelli, the son of a Florentine sculptor, improvised with stucco (for lack of enough stone). He added bold statues, arched windows, contrasting columns, a variety of forms and a shock of colour. He used the slanting northern light with stunning effect, bouncing it off a building that is half European half Russian. The Winter Palace could exist nowhere else in the world—which might be a fair criterion for any architect's success.

Since the early 19th century, the city's symbol has been the **Admiralty Tower** (Адмиралтейство—*admiralteystvo*), a golden spire surmounted by a weathervane in the form of a **61** boat. Peter the Great laid the foundation of a naval shipyard on the spot in 1704. The Admiralty that followed about a century later is a majestic, neo-classical landmark in pale yellow. The building is constructed around a massive yet graceful arch on which statues, friezes, columns and clocks crowd together illogically but impressively.

Another distinctive feature of the Leningrad skyline is the nearby **St. Isaac's Cathedral** (Исаакиевский собор—*isaakyevskiy sobor*), with its vast gold cupola surrounded by statues of angels. Its controversial French architect, Auguste Montferrand, seems to have been inspired by St. Peter's of Rome. Hampered by an unstable foundation, construction of this church (one of the world's largest) dragged on for 40 years and involved nearly half a million workmen.

The interior of St. Isaac's is cluttered with artistic and religious treasures. Scarcely an inch of wall or ceiling is left unoccupied by paintings or gold adornments. In 1931 the cathedral was converted into a museum. Legends explain the outstanding paintings, mosaics and sculptures, identifying the "incidents from Christian mythology" that are illustrated. Hardy tourists can climb to the balcony of the dome for Leningrad's best

Ceremonial arch on Palace Square connects former czarist military HQ with foreign ministry.

panoramic view. However, photography from this vantage point is forbidden for reasons of military security.

Between St. Isaac's and the river, classical buildings border Decembrists' Square (Площадь Декабристов —*ploshchad' dekabristov*), named in honour of the revolutionaries who were gunned down here in December 1825. One of Russia's unforgettable statues distinguishes this square, the **Bronze Horseman** by Etienne Falconet, also known as Peter the Great's monument.

At the Admiralty Arch

begins Leningrad's most celebrated street—the **Nevsky
Prospekt** (Невский проспект
—*nevskiy prospekt*), St. Petersburg's main artery since it was
laid out through the marshes
in the time of Peter the
Great. Running from west
to east, the three-mile-long

boulevard ends at the Alexander Nevsky Monastery.
After the Bolshevik Revolution, zealous bureaucrats tried
to change the name of the

*St. Peter's in Rome inspired
the architecture of Leningrad's
St. Isaac's Cathedral.*

street to October Prospekt, but the idea had to be abandoned when everyone ignored the decree. The Nevsky was too much a part of the city. It is a unique boulevard, a delight for the walker and the gawker, lined with stores, churches, monuments, palaces, cinemas and bridges—always throbbing with life.

The biggest church on the avenue, like St. Isaac's reminiscent of St. Peter's in Rome, is the **Cathedral of Our Lady of Kazan** (Казанский собор—*kazanskiy sobor*). A semicircular colonnade of 136 Corinthian columns encompasses pleasant gardens in front of the church. Completed in 1811, the cathedral has not only been "deconsecrated", it has been turned into a Museum of the History of Religion and Atheism. Exhibits stress the evils of the Inquisition and seek to disprove famous religious "miracles".

Sooner or later, everyone visiting Leningrad braves the crowds at **Gostinny Dvor,** the principal department store on the Nevsky Prospekt. This two-storeyed warren of boutiques may have made more sense in 1785, when it opened for business. Rebuilt at the end of the 19th century, it enabled several hundred small shopkeepers to rub elbows in a central location. Now it's run by the state. The displays are unimpressive, the service unsmiling, but this bizarre bazaar opens tourist eyes to the consumer age in the USSR.

Two other artistic and architectural attractions are to be found along the Nevsky. First, cutting across the small park of Ostrovsky Square, imperiously dominated by a statue of Catherine the Great, you come to the Pushkin Theatre (Театр имени Пушкина —*teatr imeni pushkina*), a classical effort by Rossi. You must go behind the theatre, however, to see the architect's real masterpiece: a street so perfect that merely being there brings you a sense of well-being. Identical, elegant two-storeyed houses face each other across a long, straight street—its width is exactly the same as the height of the buildings. This triumph of city planning, formerly known as Theatre Street, has been renamed **Architect Rossi Street** (Улица зодчего Росси—*ulitsa zodchevo rossi*).

Sightseers ranging further afield will discover a modern **65**

Leningrad spread all around the historic inner core. Not everything new is in memorably good taste but the worst excesses of Moscow architecture in the 1940s and 1950s were resisted. Leningrad has a metro, too. The cheerful stations are less overpowering than Moscow's palatial underground halls.

Relics of revolution may be found all over Leningrad. Hundreds of places are identified with Lenin himself, among them the Finland Station (Финляндский вокзал—*finlyandskiy vokzal*)—where his train from Finland arrived in 1917—and Smolny Institute (Смольный институт—*smol'niy institut*), designed for the daughters of the nobility, where the Bolsheviks lived and worked during the most crucial days of their revolution.

Both the outskirts and the centre of the city disclose poignant reminders of Leningrad's wartime trauma. At the beginning of the Nevsky Prospekt, a blue-and-white plaque still affixed to an official building reads:

CITIZENS!
DURING SHELLING
THIS SIDE OF STREET
IS MORE DANGEROUS

This World War II relic understates the two-and-a-half-year siege and what it meant to every Leningrad family. You can begin to imagine the scale of that ordeal at **Piskarevsky Cemetery** (Пискаревское кладбище—*piskaryovskoye kladbishche*) in the north-eastern section of the city. Though mass tragedy is incomprehensible, your heart will begin to understand as you walk between the mounds of grass covering the remains of 470,000 human beings who died of hunger, cold or bombs. As muted, mournful music filters from the loudspeakers, bereaved visitors lay flowers at the eternal flame or before the giant statue representing the Motherland.

Museums and Galleries

The Hermitage
(Эрмитаж—*ermitazh*)
If you had a week to spare in Leningrad, you might profitably spend all of it in the Hermitage and just begin to cover the marvels on view in its 400 halls. If, like most tourists, you only have time for one or two visits, consider it the

LENINGRAD
(ЛЕНИНГРАД)

barest introduction to this wondrous museum.

The Hermitage contains more than two million items ranging from prehistoric artefacts to classics of modern art, from Peter the Great's throne to a hall plastered with the portraits of 332 Russian generals. If you tackle this museum without a plan, you are almost certain to wind up both exhausted and confused. This is one place where you would be

It is difficult to decide which is the more impressive, the Hermitage itself or the splendid works of art it contains.

better off with an Intourist excursion.

Your tour is likely to begin near the top of the ceremonial staircase, in the department devoted to Russian culture—as far back as the 6th century. Conspicuous here are heroic poses of Peter the Great. The Throne Room wall is covered by a map of the USSR constructed of semiprecious stones with rubies and emeralds representing geographical features.

Back on the first floor*, the section on primitive culture presents the discoveries of Soviet archaeologists and their Russian predecessors. Very special here is a section on Scythian art of the 6th century B.C., featuring gold sculptures of striking, timeless beauty.

Parts of the second and third floors—fully 141 rooms —are given over to treasures of western European art. This is the collection acquired by seven czars, supplemented by confiscations of private collections after the revolution. (One Moscow merchant alone was relieved of 27 paintings by Matisse and 31 Picassos.)

The western European section begins on the second floor with the Italian school. Among the highlights: two madonnas by Leonardo da Vinci and Michelangelo's sculpture of the *Crouching Boy*. The Spanish department, though small, contains fine works by El Greco, Velásquez

---

*Unlike most of Europe, *first* floor means *ground* floor in the Soviet Union.

and Murillo. The large Dutch section boasts dozens of Rembrandts. The German works include Dürer, Cranach and Holbein. Reynolds and Gainsborough top the English section.

But for many visitors the most unexpected highlight is the sprawling French exhibit— from Nicholas Poussin and Claude Lorrain, Watteau and Fragonard, through Delacroix, Corot and Rodin to the treasure-trove of Impressionist and post-Impressionist works. On the third floor, room after room reveals an astonishing hoard of canvases by Pissarro, Degas, Bonnard, Monet, Derain and Toulouse-Lautrec. Here are Renoir, Van Gogh, Gauguin, Cézanne and Matisse.

And as for Picasso, the Hermitage owns a simply astonishing collection of his early works. For years much of it was kept under cover by guardians of Soviet aesthetics who feared that cubism and abstraction might undermine the people's devotion to Socialist Realism. Even in recent times the authorities expurgated the modern art display in the Hermitage, underplaying it in the official literature.

The Hermitage Museum is closed on Mondays. Tuesday to Saturday it is open 10.30 a.m. (11 in winter) to 6 p.m. and half-day Sundays.

Other Museums

After the immensity of the Hermitage, the **Russian Museum** (Русский музей—*russkiy' muzey*) is a relief: it can be explored in one painless outing.

The first four rooms of the museum contain an overwhelming collection of ancient Russian art going back to the 10th century. There are wood carvings and fragments of frescoes and mosaics. Above all, see the treasury of icons by the greatest medieval master, Andrei Rublev.

The museum is laid out chronologically from the earliest Russian religious portraits to the Agitprop era of Soviet art.

Attached to the museum is a change-of-pace gallery devoted to folk and applied art, from old Russian handicrafts to contemporary ceramics and glassware of the Soviet republics.

The Russian Museum is open daily from 10 a.m. to 6 p.m., but is closed Tuesdays. (Most Leningrad muse-

Leonardo da Vinci's unforgettable Madonna Litta.

ums close one weekday and the afternoon preceding.)

Leningrad, of course, is uniquely rich in museums and exhibitions concerned with the Bolshevik Revolution. For instance, more than 200 different locations in the city are relevant to the life of Lenin;

three houses in which he lived before the revolution are now memorial museums. The main **Lenin Museum** (Музей Ленина—*muzey lenina*) occupies Count Orlov's elegant house, the Marble Palace (completed in 1785). In the courtyard stands the armoured car from which Lenin addressed his followers at the Finland Station in April 1917.

Alongside the river, the **Dmitri Mendeleev Museum** 71

(Музей Менделеева—*muzey mendeleeva*) commemorates the Russian who discovered the periodic table of elements more than a hundred years ago, laying the groundwork for modern chemistry.

Another Russian pace-setter in the world of science, Ivan Pavlov—discoverer of the conditioned reflex—died in Leningrad in 1936. The apartment where he lived and worked for 18 years is now a museum.

After art, history and science, you may be too museum-weary to explore all the small museums and monuments devoted to the cultural sons of Leningrad. But don't forget that the musicians Glinka, Rimsky-Korsakov, Mussorgsky, Borodin and Tchaikovsky all lived in this city. Pushkin, Gogol, Goncharov, Turgenev, Dostoevsky and Gorky were among the many writers who lived and worked for a time in Leningrad. The **Museum of Russian Literary History** (Музей Истории русской литературы—*muzey istorii russkoy literatury*) assembles under one roof mementos of Tolstoy, Dostoevsky and other immortals.

Day Trips from Leningrad

With prodigious dedication and expenditure, the Soviets have restored the most lavish palaces of the czars. In some cases, these relics have been rebuilt almost from the ground up after the devastation of World War II. Three imperial estates are among Intourist's day trips from Leningrad.

The outstanding outing, 32 kilometres west of the city, takes in the dazzling opulence of **Petrodvorets** (Петродворец—*petrodvorets*). You can sign up for an Intourist guided tour or travel on your own by train, bus or—in summer—hydrofoil.

Arriving at Petrodvorets from the sea gives you the advantage of perspective. First you come to a green avenue skirting a canal. This leads up to a series of ascending fountains, a stunning staircase topped by a grandiose **palace,** painted Leningrad yellow with white trim.

Off to one side of the main palace is **Mon Plaisir** (Монплезир—*monplezir*), an intimate palace in the Dutch style so favoured by Peter I. And in the

opposite direction, you find the **Palace of Marly** (Дворец Марли—*dvorets marli*), Peter's favourite. From here, he would survey with satisfaction the Baltic fleet he had created.

Pushkin (Пушкин) is the new name of Tsarskoe Selo, a town 32 kilometres south of Leningrad. The great poet studied at the local school

Grand Cascade at Petrodvorets: brilliant achievement in opulence.

which in part explains the town's change of name. The major interest here is the regal park containing two palaces: one baroque and the other classical. Between them are statues, monuments, foun- **73** tains, gardens, ponds and lakes. Today's Soviets promenade through it all with pride in Russia's rich traditions, re-created here at almost limitless expense.

Just 6 kilometres east of the town of Pushkin, **Pavlovsk** (Павловск) is another summer palace to see. Intourist bites them off separately on the sensible grounds that nobody could absorb two such expeditions in one day. Catherine the Great presented Pavlovsk to her eccentric son Paul in 1777. The park, formal and forested, runs to some 1,300 acres.

On the road between Leningrad and Pushkin and Pavlovsk you cross the main line of wartime resistance, the limit to which the German forces advanced in their attempts to take the city. A granite obelisk marks the siege line.

About 1 kilometre away, you'll notice the white domes of the Pulkovo Observatory (Пулковская обсерватория —*pulkovskaya observatoriya*). Established in 1838 and reconstructed after wartime destruction, Pulkovo determines the exact time beeped by Radio Moscow. Scientists, but not ordinary tourists, may arrange visits.

What to Do

Shopping

No tourist worth his baggage-tag collection wants to return home without a quota of souvenirs. Russia has good pickings, from frivolous and cheap to artistic and emphatically expensive. Finding off-beat items requires patience and persistence so the shopper on the run may have to settle for fairly standard souvenirs.

The big stores are strong on pots and pans, sofas and curtains, and other goods more exciting for the locals than the tourists. But you ought to look through one or two of these institutions in case something

Get in There and Shop
In most Soviet stores, buying is a three-stage operation:

1. When you see what you want to purchase, memorize the price.

2. Find the cashier, wherever she may be in the store, and pay the exact amount.

3. Present your receipt back at the original sales counter and point to what you have bought.

You may have to queue and jostle at each point. Stand up for your rights.

strikes you. Just mingling with the mainstream of the Soviet consumer society amounts to an intangible bonus.

The best known of Moscow's department stores is GUM (ГУМ) smack on Red Square. Three hundred and fifty thousand shoppers cram this rambling emporium every day.

TSUM (ЦУМ) is GUM's big competitor, virtually next door to the Bolshoi Theatre.

Cobbler tries to keep warm in his stall on Moscow street corner. He sells shoelaces for every taste and can do most repairs in minutes.

Each matryoshka *doll houses a whole family of dolls in decreasing sizes.*

The biggest, best-known ordinary (rouble) store in Leningrad is Gostinny Dvor (Гостиный Двор), the enormous arcaded building at 15, Nevsky Prospekt. This conglomeration of small shops (all state-owned) sells little in the way of Western-style luxuries, but plenty of pots and pans, pins, pens and purses. Amble through the clothing departments for a grass-roots survey of Soviet style and prices.

Certain shops cater only to the foreign tourists and diplomats. Most of these are called Beryozka (''Берёзка''), meaning ''little birch tree''. Beryozka shops quote prices in roubles but the goods must be paid for in the equivalent amount of pounds sterling, U.S. dollars or almost any other Western currency—*never* in roubles. Because the throngs of ordinary Soviet shoppers are barred, Beryozka shops are less hectic. Quite a few of the items aren't available in ordinary shops, and the prices are often attractive. It's tempting to confine your buying spree to these duty-free areas where the salespeople usually speak foreign languages. But don't miss the experience of shopping with roubles at GUM or TSUM or at least window-shopping along Gorky Street or the Nevsky Prospekt.

What to Buy

Without any money-back guarantees, here are some suggestions on what to *consider* buying. Remember the old Russian saying: each to his own taste.

Amber. Bracelets, necklaces and other specialities of the Baltic republics.

Books. You don't have to know the language to buy the picture books of Soviet cities and museum treasures, very economically priced. When available, they're sold at hotel bookstalls.

Caviar. Prices have gone out of sight, but even so, sturgeon eggs still sell by the jar and not by the dozen. Purchases plus receipt must be presented to customs on departure.

Cameras. Photo and home-movie fans report enthusias-tically about the Soviet cameras on sale around town, particularly the low prices at Beryozkas.

Dolls. The most familiar are the *matryoshka* wooden dolls, hidden one inside another almost to infinity. For a fascinating survey of Soviet toys, spend an hour wandering Detsky Mir ("Детский мир"), or "children's world". This department store for tots and teens may be found in Dzerzhinsky Square in Moscow, alongside Lubyanka, the traditional headquarters of the secret police.

Embroidery. Those Ukrainian blouses are much admired. Lacework from northern Russia also turns up at large Beryozkas.

Fur hats. For every pocket and for most heads; a splendidly typical, useful Russian souvenir. The ones with convertible earmuffs, formerly for men only, are now thought chic for women.

Glass-holders. Fragile, ornately designed metal handles to attach to your glass of piping-hot tea; no overweight baggage problems here. Most Beryozkas stock them.

Lacquered boxes. The best-known are from Palekh, a

small central Russian town whose craftsmen painted icons for four centuries until the revolution, when they switched to papier-mâché boxes. The designs are original, the colour and detail inimitable. They come in many shapes, sizes and prices—cigarette cases, jewellery boxes, pill-boxes.

Musical instruments. How about a balalaika or a cheap guitar?

Posters. When Soviet artists plunged into revolutionary propaganda, they produced many modern classics of poster art. These, and the extravagantly anti-capitalist, anti-imperialist Agitprop posters make bright wall decorations.

Records. Whether you want to remember your trip with a Shostakovich symphony or the Red Army Chorus, records are nicely priced souvenirs. An off-beat gift might be the latest Moscow top-of-the-pops.

Rugs. Centuries-old designs from Soviet Central Asia, such as the famous Bukhara rugs, are favourites. Excess baggage assessments may be a problem.

Scents. Soviet perfumes (with names like Red Moscow) have never frightened the French competition but they make an inexpensive novelty gift. Many souvenir shops stock them.

Stamps. Any stamp-collector you know at home will appreciate the everyday oddities of Soviet postage stamps. They come in unusual shapes and sizes with plenty of bright colours and vigorous designs.

Vodka. Enthusiasts argue whether Stolichnaya (Столичная) or Moskovskaya (Московская) is the real thing. You may want to try pepper vodka or other arcane variations. At duty-free locations, including the airport, the great Russian distillate is a spirited bargain to take home.

Watches. The kind the cosmonauts wear, as the commercials say, are stylish and real bargains.

Wooden spoons, bowls, trays and what-not from the village of Khokhloma: bright red and gold traditional designs passed down from father to son for centuries; surprisingly, they're usable and washable. Sold at souvenir stands everywhere.

The major shops are usually open from 8 or 9 a.m. to 8 or 9 p.m. daily, Monday to Saturday, with an hour-long lunch break.

Relaxing

If you have visions of a groovy nightlife scene, you must be thinking of those murky Russian nightclubs in Paris. In Moscow, Leningrad and all other Soviet cities the situation isn't what you would call racy. In view of the official staid morality, evenings out tend to be wholesome and relatively early so that everyone can turn up at the factory next morning.

The good news, however, is

Leningrad's Kirov Theatre is a tourist attraction in itself.

that the theatre and music scene is lively and inexpensive. And while restaurants close early, fun-loving Russians turn a baroque dining hall into a party, dancing and all.

As if that weren't enough, foreigners are permitted to carouse after midnight in special hard-currency bars. They tend to be very stuffy, gloomy places, for that's the way the Russians imagine a Western cocktail bar ought to feel.

Three arts festivals are organized each year in the USSR:

Moscow: "Moscow Stars" (May 5–13), "Russian Winter" (Dec. 25–Jan. 5);

Leningrad: "White Nights" (June 21–29).

Opera, ballet and symphonic productions are presented for these festivals. Intourist sells package tours which include theatre tickets.

Ballet, Concerts, Theatre

Dozens of splendid theatres and concert halls maintain a praiseworthy standard of opera, ballet, symphony, drama and folk dancing. Weekly lists of all attractions are posted at hotel service desks. Intourist can wave its magic wand and obtain tickets to many plays and concerts at short notice. But even Intourist's influence can't add to the 2,150 seats at the Bolshoi, Moscow's most celebrated theatre. So don't be shattered if no tickets are left for *Swan Lake* in its classic setting.

Actually, the artists of the Bolshoi (meaning "great" or "grand" or just plain "big" in Russian) frequently move to the huge stage of the Kremlin Palace of Congresses. This modern hall seats 6,000 with obvious improvement in the odds for tickets. You'll do well to look in on the Palace's snack-bar between the acts—if you can call smoked salmon and champagne a snack.

Especially when the Bolshoi is out of town, touring companies often perform.

Another strength of the Moscow scene is the quality of the concerts. World-renowned Soviet musicians perform in the stately surroundings of the Conservatory of Music (Консерватория—*konservatoriya*), Tchaikovsky Hall (Зал Чайковского—*zal chaykovskovo*) and the Hall of Columns of Trade Union House (Колонный зал Дома Союзов—*kolonniy zal doma soyuzov*).

If you know Russian you'll want to go to the theatre—perhaps the Maly (Малый театр —*maliy teatr*), the "small" one, across the square from the Bolshoi or the Moscow Art Theatre (Московский художественный театр—*moskovskiy khudozhestvenniy teatr*) of Stanislavsky fame (with a new theatre of architectural note). Even if you don't know the language, consider sitting in on a Russian translation of Shakespeare or Shaw, for the mood, method and colour, if not the words.

The Central Puppet Theatre (Центральный театр кукол —*central'niy teatr kukol*) may be another solution to the language barrier. Although it's primarily for children, adult foreigners feel right at home.

Leningrad's most renowned theatre, the Kirov (Театр имени Кирова—*teatr imeni kirova*), is worth visiting no matter what's playing. The auditorium itself is a magnificent five-tiered gilt horseshoe—all plush and crystal, with flying angels to top it all off. The building (the Mariinsky Theatre before the revolution) was badly damaged during the war. But renovations began even before the siege had lifted, and concerts resumed on September 1, 1944.

The Kirov's ballet corps of 200, chorus of 100 and orchestra of more than 100 are tops by any world standard. Anna Pavlova danced here,

Russian Composers

Russia's greatest 19th-century composers began their careers in uniform—as government clerks or junior military officers.

MIKHAIL GLINKA (1804–57), who endured four years at the Ministry of Communications, wrote the stirring opera *Ivan Susanin*, sometimes known as *A Life for the Czar*.

MODEST MUSSORGSKY (1839–81), briefly an officer of the guard and for many years a civil-service clerk, composed Russia's great nationalist opera, *Boris Godunov*.

PETER ILYICH TCHAIKOVSKY (1840–93) was employed as a senior clerk in the Justice Ministry before writing eleven operas, six symphonies, three immortal ballets *(Swan Lake, Sleeping Beauty, The Nutcracker)* and a cannon-roaring *(1812)* overture.

NIKOLAI RIMSKY-KORSAKOV (1844–1908) composed his first symphony aboard ship as a naval cadet. While Inspector of Naval Bands, he wrote evocative symphonic poems: *Scheherazade* and *Capriccio Espagnol*.

81

Chaliapin sang here and many famous ballet dancers, including Ulanova and Rudolf Nureyev, began their careers here. Whether they're doing *Boris Godunov* or the *Queen of Spades* (both were premiered on this stage), or even a Socialist Realism rouser on the joys of collective farming, don't miss the chance. The theatre seats 1,752 (note the extra-wide armchairs specially designed to fit Russian anatomies).

If the ticket situation is hopeless, or the Kirov closed for the week, don't be dismayed. Leningrad's second most-honoured company, the Maly Opera Theatre (Малый Оперный театр—*maliy operniy teatr*) is probably performing something superb. The theatre itself, like the Kirov, is a baroque delight, and the music and dance are inevitably first class. Still on musical themes, Tchaikovsky's old

Classical ballet at the summit: Giselle *at the Bolshoi. Moscow's most celebrated theatre seats only 2,150, so book as early as possible.*

home town usually has several good concerts and recitals. The Philharmonic Society operates two concert halls, on and just off the Nevsky Prospekt.

Language is no big handicap at the Musical Comedy Theatre (Театр Музыкальной комедии—*teatr muzykal'noy komedii*), which performs mostly operettas. There, too, the spare-no-expense staging is something to see.

Circus

Universally appealing, the Moscow Circus (Московский цирк—*moskovskiy tsirk*) fills its single ring with spectacles seen nowhere else. It's especially strong on startling animal acts. The unique Russian performing bears are a special treat; as for the clowns, laughter is an international language.

Bears on ice-skates—no joke!—figure among the oddities of Circus on Ice (Цирк на льду—*tsirk na l'du*), a variation on familiar themes.

Skill and precision—hallmarks of Moscow Circus artists.

Leningrad also supports a puppet theatre and a major circus (Ленинградскнй цирк —*leningradskiy tsirk*), which you don't have to be a child to appreciate.

Films

If you run out of things to do, the cinemas operate from morning to late evening. All films have a Russian soundtrack. Once a film starts, though, nobody can enter.

Mosfilm and other Soviet studios provide most of the attractions.

Sports

Sports fans, on the other hand, will thrill to Russian-style football (soccer), athletic events, ice-hockey and horse races. Muscovites take their football as seriously as any sports fans in the world. For the flavour of big-time competition, try to see a match at Dynamo Stadium (стадион 'Динамо'—*stadion dinamo*), on Leningrad Boulevard. Luzhniki Park, which includes Lenin Stadium, is often the scene of international competitions. Moscow's Hippodrome (ипподром—*ippodrom*) on Begovaya Street just off Leningrad Boulevard, is different from any track you've attended. There's harness and thoroughbred racing with low-stake pari-mutuel betting.

Leningrad enjoys all manner of athletic facilities, from neighbourhood hockey rinks to the 100,000-seat Kirov Stadium.

Diversions range from sensational sword act to old-fashioned "troika" rides.

Wining and Dining

A highlight of eating out in Russia is a hard one for the tourist to miss. It's the dine-and-dance scene which most major hotel restaurants provide as a festive night out. Everything but the rules of dress is formal: shimmering chandeliers, starched table-cloths, arrays of crystal at the ready. As the small orchestra strikes up, you know you're set for hours of gaiety. The stress, though, may be on "hours". The concept of speedy service is quite foreign to Russian waiters. If you concede this in advance and prepare yourself to coexist with the problem, a good time may be had by all.

(A recent innovation at certain hotels is the introduction of a separate dining room for "express service", meaning self-service. But it's an isolated phenomenon, still in the experimental stage.)

Reserve your table in advance through a Russian-speaking person or the Intourist service desk: Russians plan evenings out as *entire* evenings. So it may be hopeless to wait patiently in the expecta-

tion that a couple of seats will become vacant before the lights dim at closing time. For the record, Intourist meal vouchers are valid not only in your own hotel but in any Intourist establishment. They've a specific cash value in roubles and may be combined any way you want to pay for food and drink. That is, if your bill comes to more than the value of one dinner voucher (which is quite likely), add a breakfast ticket, and you may get change in kopeks.

Under the economic reforms of the late 1980s, new, cooperatively run restaurants revolutionized the dining-out scene. But be prepared to pay heavily for the novelty of fine food and courteous service.

Most hotels have standard menus printed in four languages. Don't let the encyclopedic style overwhelm you. The only items actually available are those with a price listed. From one of those universal menu books, we've chosen highlights of Russian cuisine worth trying.

Appetizers

The best often comes first in a Russian meal so you're well advised to dig in to the hors d'oeuvre. Caviar (икра—*ikra*) is an acquired and alarmingly expensive taste. When available, it's generally served with toast, butter and a slice of lemon. Black roe comes from sturgeon, red from salmon.

Fishy starters. The Russians, like the Scandinavians, enjoy the combination of cold fish and chilled alcohol. Smoked salmon, jellied sturgeon or pickled herring hit the spot with a shot of vodka.

Salads. A popular salad is composed of a sumptuous mound of diced potatoes, cucumber, carrots, onion, peas, chicken, ham and hard-boiled egg folded into a rich creamy dressing. In the West, it may be known as Russian salad but the Soviet name is салат столичный *(salat stolichniy),* "capital city" salad.

"Hot refreshments", as restaurant menus describe these delicacies, fit halfway between appetizers and a whole meal. For instance, thinly sliced chicken or meat, served in individual casseroles, is a subtle first course pleasant to several of the senses. In Russian it's called *julienne.* Then there are mushrooms in sour cream (грибы в сметане—*gribi v sme-*

tane), and considering the Russian love affair with mushrooms and sour cream, this is a favourite dish if there ever was one. It should be eaten with that hearty, healthful black bread.

Soups

If you haven't eaten too much with the first couple of courses, try an old-fashioned Russian soup.

Borsht (борщ). The name is famous and flexible; the recipe varies greatly from kitchen to kitchen. In Soviet restaurants, basically, it's a hot beetroot and cabbage soup with chunks of boiled meat and a dab of sour cream to temper the sweet-and-sour overtones. It's often served with a delicate cheese pie on the side.

Bouillon (бульон—*bulyon*). Sounds too simple but Russian chicken broth can be served with more than the predictable noodles or croutons. One beloved variation is a rich broth with dumplings. Called пельмени *(pel'meni),* these are prepared with chopped meat wrapped in thin noodle dough. The dumplings can also be merely served on a plate as a main course with a dash of vinegar or sour cream.

Okroshka (окрошка). A summertime soup, served chilled, this exotic dish is unlikely to provoke love at first taste, but it's worth a try. The secret ingredient is kvass, a slightly alcoholic drink fermented from black bread. The soup's ingredients can run from cucumbers, onions and hard-boiled egg to a sliver of meat.

Fish Dishes

Although Soviet trawlers ply many seas, the typical Moscow or Leningrad menu limits fish dishes to only a couple of species: usually pike-perch and sturgeon. The cooks do well with what they have, starting with fish and chips with tartar sauce. More exotic recipes cover baked or steamed fish with tangy cream sauces. Another item, listed in the English translation of one menu as "sturgeon on spits", turns out to be fish kebab or grilled, skewered fish.

Meat Dishes

Caucasian shashlik (шашлык), though hardly a local invention, is a popular Russian restaurant dish. Skewered pieces of mutton and onion are grilled over the embers and served with a hot sauce.

classic of Russian cuisine. Thin strips of beef tenderloin are braised in a sauce of mushrooms, onions and sour cream.

An unfortunate menu translation for a beef stew in the Russian style reads "stewed beet (sic!) with culinary roots".

For the record, the way to say beefsteak in Russian is *bifshteks*. It's usually fried and served with fried onions or fried eggs and chips (French fries).

Two unique dishes commend themselves:

Chicken Kiev (котлеты по-киевски—*kotleti po-kiyevski*) sounds Ukrainian, not Russian, but who could argue over such a bird? Boned chicken breasts are filled with melted butter. Careful how you handle it with a knife and fork to avoid splattering.

Chicken tabaka (цыплята табака—*tsiplyata tabaka*). It's Georgian, not Russian, but extremely popular with Muscovites. Salted and peppery, the bird is flattened onto a buttered skillet and slowly done until crisp. Chopped onion on the side and a hot, garlic sauce are optional for an oriental accent.

Lyulya-kebab(люлякебаб), a variation, consists of skewered meatballs called "cutlets in oriental style".

Beef Stroganov (беф-строганов), named after the family which won the salt-mine concession from Ivan the **88** Terrible, must be the all-time

Desserts

The Russians have a highly developed sweet tooth, so tourists may have to be brave to resist overfulfilling the calory norm. Ice-cream was definitely *not* invented by the Russians but they've made admirable advances in its refinement. The major restaurants compete for the most elaborate version of sundaes with fruit and biscuits (cookies).

Surprise or Siberian Omelet (омлет "Сюрприз" or сибирский омлет—*omlet syurpriz/sibirskiy omlet*) is known in other longitudes as Norwegian omelet or baked Alaska.

Pastries. The quality fluctuates so you may want to wait till you're in a tea or coffee shop and choose by sight. Some vocabulary: *tort* (торт) means a tart or a cake. *Keks* (кекс) means a sponge cake. *Romovaya baba* (ромовая баба) is a cake steeped in rum syrup.

Blini (блины) quite resemble the blintzes served up in American delicatessens. These airy pancakes come last on our

Kremlin Palace of Congresses' buffet is reputed to serve the finest delicacies in Moscow.

list, though in actual Russian life, they may be eaten anytime during the meal or as a snack. As a first course, *blini* are made with caviar or smoked salmon and of course the requisite dollop of sour cream. The dessert variation, called оладьи *(oladyi)*, is smaller, served in tandem with jam or cottage cheese and dusted with confectioner's sugar.

Beverages

In the more elegant Soviet restaurants you may find as many as half a dozen glasses of various sizes and shapes arrayed at each place setting. Every glass has a particular purpose. Don't be self-conscious about pouring water into your wine glass. It's much more vital to remember never to drink vodka on an empty stomach.

This prohibition should be a fairly obvious safety precaution. But in addition, Russians consider it uncouth to take a nip before consuming at least a mouthful or two of food—even if it's only black bread. Another social ordinance: before downing each round, it's virtually obligatory to raise your glass in a toast to your neighbours at the table.

Vodka (водка), it ought to be mentioned, is drunk chilled, straight down the hatch, not mixed. The concept of the vodka Martini, the Screwdriver or vodka tonic —mastered in cocktail lounges for foreigners—is unheard of in ordinary Soviet circles. In restaurants vodka is never served by the glass, always by weight. One hundred grams, about three and a half ounces, or a double measure for us, is the size of the minimum flask generally available.

The other tiny stemmed glass on your table is reserved for brandy (коньяк—*konyak*). The Russians persist in using the generic term "cognac" even though it upsets the Cognac producers of France. Armenia and Georgia provide the best Soviet brandy, some of it excellent by any standard. Some Russians actually drink brandy at the beginning of a meal instead of saving it for last.

Shampanskoye (шампанское) is the Russian word for a domestic sparkling white wine the French would probably call sham champagne. For an imitation, it's exceedingly good. Connoisseurs of Soviet bubbly advocate the dry (*suk-*

hoye—сухое) or slightly dry (*polusukhoye*—полусухое).

Soviet table wines are well regarded. They've numbers as well as names which helps anyone who can't decipher the incredible Georgian alphabet. No. 1 is *Tsinandali* (цинандали), a refreshing dry white wine. No. 4 is *Mukuzani* (мукузани), a full-bodied red. If these two are available, forget about learning any other numbers.

Mineral water holds an honoured place on Soviet tables. If you can get it, *Narzan* (нарзан) fizzes tastily.

As Soviet consumers become more demanding, restaurant managers are trying to improve atmosphere, service and quality of cooking.

Borzhom (боржом), more commonly available, is so good for you that its heavy mineral taste may put you off.

Fruit juice, lemonade and fruit drinks supplement the soft-drink list in restaurants.

If one glass is still dry, it may be reserved for beer. The Soviet product is a bit flat. Fortunately, imported pilsener is usually available.

Rounding out the beverage survey, it should be mentioned that coffee isn't a Russian speciality. However, it's occasionally possible to find "Eastern coffee", the Soviet version of Turkish coffee—strongly flavoured but, if you're a devotee, tasty.

Tea, authentically Russian, is a better bet anywhere in the USSR.

To Help You Order...

Could we have a table...?	Пожалуйста столик...	*pozhaluysta stolik*
Do you have a set menu?	Есть ли у вас комплексные обеды?	*yest' li u vas kompleksniye obedi*
I'd like a/an/some...	Принесите, пожалуйста...	*prinesite pozhaluysta*
beer	пива	*piva*
bread	хлеба	*khleba*
coffee	кофе	*kofe*
fish	рыбу	*ribu*
fruit	фруктов	*fruktov*
glass	стакан	*stakan*
meat	мясо	*myaso*
menu	меню	*myenyu*
milk	молока	*moloka*
mineral water	минеральной воды	*minyeral'noy vodi*
napkin	салфетку	*salfyetku*
salad	салат	*salat*
sandwich	бутерброд	*butyerbrod*
serviette	салфетку	*salfyetku*
soup	супу	*supu*
sugar	сахару	*sakharu*
tea	чаю	*chayu*
wine	вина	*vina*

...and Read the Menu

апельсины	*apyel'sini*	oranges
беф-строганов	*bef-stroganof*	beef Stroganoff
бифштекс	*bifshteks*	beefsteak
битки	*bitki*	meatballs
блины	*blini*	pancakes
говядина	*govyadina*	beef
ветчина	*vetchina*	ham
грибы	*gribi*	mushrooms
икра	*ikra*	caviar
картофель	*kartofyel'*	potatoes
капуста	*kapusta*	cabbage
колбаса	*kolbasa*	cold cuts
котлеты по-киевски	*kotlyeti po kiyevski*	butter-stuffed chicken breasts
крабы	*krabi*	crab
курица	*kuritsa*	chicken
лимон	*limon*	lemon
морковь	*morkov'*	carrots
мороженое	*morozhenoye*	ice-cream
осётр	*osyotr*	sturgeon
огурец	*ogurets*	cucumber
персики	*persiki*	peaches
пирожные	*pirozhniye*	pastry
помидоры	*pomidori*	tomatoes
рис	*ris*	rice
ростбиф	*rostbif*	roast beef
салат	*salat*	salad
свинина	*svinina*	pork
сельдь	*syel'd'*	herring
семга	*syomga*	salmon
сыр	*sir*	cheese
сосиски	*sosiski*	sausage
судак	*sudak*	pike-perch
телятина	*tyelyatina*	veal
утка	*utka*	duck
форель	*forel'*	trout
цыплёнок	*tsiplyonok*	chicken
шашлык	*shashlik*	shashlik
щука	*shchuka*	pike
язык	*yazik*	tongue
яйца	*yaytsa*	eggs

BLUEPRINT for a Perfect Trip

How to Get There

In spite of the numbers of visitors to the USSR in recent years, the room supply isn't *always* equal to the demand—especially in summer. Above all, make your hotel (or camping) arrangements *early*. You cannot get a visa until your accommodation is reserved and paid for, and you cannot go to the Soviet Union without a visa.

A reliable travel agent will be able to advise on the latest prices and help you find an arrangement that fits your particular requirements.

BY AIR

Scheduled Flights

From London: there are regular, direct, non-stop flights all year round to Moscow. Connecting flights are also available from Dublin and regional airports in Britain. A few direct flights link London and Leningrad, but it's more usual to stop or change planes in Moscow, Helsinki, Stockholm or Copenhagen.

From North America: there are flights to Moscow from New York, Washington DC and Montreal through one of the European gateway cities, like London, Paris, Helsinki or Zurich.

Leningrad passengers have to change planes in Europe, chiefly Helsinki, Stockholm, Copenhagen or Amsterdam.

Regular scheduled airlines offer reduced excursion fares to Europe for passengers flying at non-peak times or staying a certain number of days.

Charter Flights and Package Tours

From the British Isles: inclusive package tours, offering flight, hotel and meals are available. Prices are advantageous since the tour operators obtain special rates because of the large number of bookings involved.

Intourist, the Soviet travel bureau, offers a variety of such inclusive tours featuring Moscow, Leningrad and other cities. Your travel agent should have details of these and other programmes.

To be on the safe side, take out cancellation insurance to cover any loss if illness or accident should prevent your departure.

From North America: cheap charter flights to Moscow exist, but they are not easy to find and are not entirely reliable. Many travellers take a charter to a point in western Europe, then continue on to Moscow, rejoining their charter on the return date.

Travel agents can offer OTC (one-stop inclusive tour charter), a package including specific hotels and other land arrangements.

BY CAR

Driving to Moscow from western Europe or following the sea/road route from the British Isles or the continent are not really practical propositions for most people: the distance and time involved are just too great.

The itinerary must be chosen and approved in advance and the necessary visa or visas acquired—which can be a lengthy process. Although it is possible to get visas at the frontier crossings, you must be prepared for all sorts of difficulties and delays.

BY RAIL

Travelling to Moscow by train from western Europe takes several days. Rail fares are cheaper than airline travel, but remember that you have to eat during the journey, and meals or snacks on trains can be expensive. Russian train carriages have samovars with free continuous hot water, so travellers can save money by bringing a supply of tea bags, instant coffee and soups.

However, if time is no problem and your aim is to see a wide variety of countries—if only through a train window—rail travel can be interesting. And it's possible to make stop-overs at numerous points along the way. From the U.K., for example, you could cross the Channel to Ostend, board a special sleeper train for Moscow, passing through Brussels, Cologne, Düsseldorf, Hannover, Berlin, Warsaw, Brest and finally Moscow. From Ostend, the trip takes about three days. Rail connections on to Leningrad are frequent (a seven- to nine-hour trip). You can also travel directly from Helsinki to Leningrad by train.

BY SEA

It is also possible to combine rail and sea travel—again if time is no problem. There are regular sailings between Hamburg and Leningrad. You can then continue your trip to Moscow either by train or by plane.

YOUTH TRAVEL IN THE USSR

In the Soviet Union, Sputnik, the Soviet youth travel association, offers reductions of 50 per cent on rail travel and (in winter only) 30 per cent on air travel. Sputnik works in collaboration with 500 youth organizations in 80 countries. For foreign youth groups they arrange organized visits to the best-known arts festivals, national and international exhibitions, language courses, etc. Contact a travel agency that cooperates with Sputnik or Intourist.

An A–Z Summary of Practical Information and Facts

> Listed after most main entries is an appropriate Russian translation and transcription, usually in the singular. You'll find this vocabulary useful when asking for assistance.

AIRPORT (аэропорт – *aeroport*). Most international flights arrive at Sheremetyevo Airport, nearly 20 miles northwest of Moscow. (Two other major airports to the south of the city—Domodedovo and Vnukovo—are used primarily for domestic services.)

Facilities at Sheremetyevo's Terminal II include a restaurant and a snack bar, shops selling newspapers and souvenirs and a duty-free shop for travellers with hard currency, a currency-exchange office, a post office, luggage deposit, cinema, nursery, Intourist information desks and a car rental counter.

A number of international airlines fly directly to Leningrad. If you go by way of Moscow, however, it's easy to catch one of Aeroflot's shuttle flights to Leningrad.

When going through customs, you fill out a customs declaration form (see CURRENCY and CUSTOMS CONTROL). After customs clearance, you must check with the Intourist desk to confirm hotel assignment and arrange for transport. Members of Intourist group tours travel free between the airport and the hotel and needn't pay porters for handling their luggage. If you are not travelling with an Intourist group, you'd do best to take a taxi into town.

ALPHABET. The exotic Cyrillic letters of the Russian alphabet needn't be a mystery to you. The alphabet is on page 98. The column at left shows printed capital and small letters while the centre column shows the same letters in handwritten form. The right-hand column shows you approximately what these letters correspond to in English. It's the basis for the simplified transliteration used in this guide. If you're more interested in getting along in the language, you'll want to get a copy of the Berlitz phrase book, RUSSIAN FOR TRAVELLERS.

A

А а	*А а*	a
Б б	*Б б*	b
В в	*В в*	v
Г г	*Г г*	g
Д д	*Д д*	d
Е е	*Е е*	e, ye
Ё ё	*Ё ё*	yo
Ж ж	*Ж ж*	zh
З з	*З з*	z
И и	*И и*	i
Й й	*Й й*	y
К к	*К к*	k
Л л	*Л л*	l
М м	*М м*	m
Н н	*Н н*	n
О о	*О о*	o
П п	*П п*	p

Р р	*Р р*	r
С с	*С с*	s
Т т	*Т т*	t
У у	*У у*	u
Ф ф	*Ф ф*	f
Х х	*Х х*	kh
Ц ц	*Ц ц*	ts
Ч ч	*Ч ч*	ch
Ш ш	*Ш ш*	sh
Щ щ	*Щ щ*	shch
Ъ ъ	*Ъ ъ*	(mute)
Ы ы	*Ы ы*	i
Ь ь	*Ь ь*	'
Э э	*Э э*	e
Ю ю	*Ю ю*	yu
Я я	*Я я*	ya

The letter ь, shown in our transcription as an apostrophe ('), gives a "soft" pronunciation to the preceding consonant. A similar effect can be produced by pronouncing *y* as in *yet*—but very, very short—after the consonant.

B **BABYSITTERS** (присмотр за детьми – *prismotr za det'mi*). In a country with traditional "built-in" babysitters—*babushkas* (grandmothers)—the problem rarely arises for Russians. But the floor attendant in your hotel should be able to organize informal facilities.

Can you get us a babysitter for tonight?	Нельзя ли найти кого-нибудь присмотреть за ребенком сегодня вечером?	*nyel'zya li nayti kovo-nibud' prismotret' za rebyonkom sevodnya vecherom*

BANKS and CURRENCY-EXCHANGE OFFICES (банк; пункт обмена валюты – *bank ; punkt obmena valyuti*). Unless you anticipate fairly elaborate financial dealings, you'll have no reason to travel as far as the Moscow Bank for Foreign Trade (Внешторгбанк – *vneshtorgbank*) at 8, Serpukhovskoy Val. It's open Monday to Friday, 9.30 a.m. to 1 p.m.

To change travellers' cheques or foreign currency into roubles, go no farther than the currency-exchange desk in your hotel. Hours vary from place to place but currency-exchange desks are open considerably longer and are easier to deal with than banks.

Remember to carry your passport and currency-control certificate when changing money.

Any "informal" (black-market) currency transactions are illegal; the Soviet authorities consider such offences very grave. Anyone caught indulging in illegal currency transactions is likely to be expelled from the country at the very least.

I want to change some pounds/dollars.	**Я хочу обменять фунты/доллары.**	*ya khochu obmenyat' funti/dollari*

BARBER'S—see HAIRDRESSER'S

BOY MEETS GIRL. Many glowing reports have been heard on the enthusiastic openness with which young Russians approach boy-girl situations. There remain, however, problems of language and logistics. Soviet hotel rooms, vigilantly defended against impropriety, are off limits, and local housing conditions make it unlikely that any love-nests are to be found. See RIVER CRUISES, p. 55.

BUS SERVICES—see PUBLIC TRANSPORT

CAMPING (кемпинг – *kemping*). During the brief summer season—June to August and, in some areas, part of September—authorized camp-sites are operated near many Soviet cities. Campers may park a car and pitch a tent for a fixed rate that includes amenities, from showers to cooking facilities, plus a guided tour of nearby attractions. At some camp-sites, bungalows are available.

Arrangements must be made in advance through travel agents outside the USSR.

CAR RENTAL (прокат автомобиля – *prokat avtomobilya*). Arrangements for hiring a car—with or without a chauffeur—can be made at the same time you book your hotel accommodation; alternatively, you can rent one on the spot through Intourist service desks at major hotels. Foreigners must pay in hard currency or with an internationally recognized credit card. An International Driving Licence is required. The minimum age is 21.

For driving conditions and regulations, see pp. 104–108.

CHURCH SERVICES (богослужение – *bogosluzheniye*). Most churches are open to the public during services only, so if you go into a historic church with a view to sightseeing, stay in the rear of the building in order not to disturb the worshippers.

Russian-Orthodox divine liturgy is conducted at a number of churches around Moscow. The seat of the patriarch is Epiphany Cathedral at Spartakovskaya Street.

Protestant church services in English are held at the British and American embassies. Roman-Catholic mass is said at the American embassy and in the Chapel of Our Lady of Hope (English and French). Contact your embassy for further details.

The Moscow Synagogue is at 8, Archipova Street. The mosque is at 7, Vypolzov Pereulok.

In Leningrad, the biggest and most interesting of the functioning Orthodox churches is St. Nicholas' Cathedral, 3, Kommunarov Square. Other religious services are held in the Roman Catholic church at 7, Kovensky Pereulok, the Baptist church at 29a, Bolshaya Ozernaya, the synagogue on Lermontovsky Prospekt and the mosque on Kirovsky Prospekt.

CIGARETTES, CIGARS, TOBACCO (сигареты, сигары, табак – *sigareti, sigari, tabak*). Soviet cigarettes, sold at stands all over town, may taste rough to the uninitiated. Several makes of American, British, French and West German cigarettes are usually on sale for hard currency in Beryozka shops and at hotels.

For a novelty smoke or a souvenir, try *papirosi*. These traditional Russian cigarettes consist of a short length of cigarette fitted onto a long, hollow cardboard holder.

Close relations between the USSR and Cuba have brought a vast supply of cigars onto the market.

Pipe smokers will find Russian tobacco exotic.

A packet of cigarettes/	**Пачка сигарет/**	*pachka sigaret/*
A pack of matches.	**Коробка спичек.**	*korobka spichek*
filter-tipped	**с фильтром**	*s fil'trom*
without filter	**без фильтра**	*bez fil'tra*
Russian stub cigarettes	**папиросы**	*papirosi*

CLIMATE and CLOTHING. Summer is short, sweet and, for the most part, comfortably warm. In all other seasons you'll be glad you brought some extra sweaters with you. Despite cold winters, temperatures *indoors* are always very warm, so layers of clothing that you can peel off are to be recommended.

As for fashion, the only taboos would be the two extremes: ostentation and way-out informality. Evening gowns with cascades of diamonds are definitely not recommended. And on the opposite fringe, it would be shockingly out of place to wear shorts in Gorky Street or Nevsky Prospekt. (Keep in mind that old-fashioned morality pervades Soviet life.)

There are only a few occasions when men would be well advised to wear a dark suit and tie and women a dress in subdued tones. These might include an invitation to meet Soviet officials or a night at the opera. But even in these cases, the Soviets around you are liable to be less formally dressed. Ties, for instance, are almost never obligatory.

Moscow:		J	F	M	A	M	J	J	A	S	O	N	D
average daily	°F	3	8	18	34	46	51	55	53	45	37	26	15
minimum*	°C	–16	–14	–8	1	8	11	13	12	7	3	–3	–10
average daily	°F	15	22	32	50	66	70	73	72	61	48	35	24
maximum*	°C	–9	–6	0	10	19	21	23	22	16	9	2	–5
Leningrad:													
average daily	°F	8	11	18	33	42	51	55	55	47	39	28	18
minimum*	°C	–13	–12	–8	0	6	11	13	13	9	4	–2	–8
average daily	°F	19	22	32	46	59	68	70	69	60	48	35	26
maximum*	°C	–7	–5	0	8	15	20	21	20	15	9	2	–3

*Minimum temperatures are measured just before sunrise, maximum temperatures in the early afternoon.

COMPLAINTS (жалобы – *zhalobi*). Intourist will politely listen to all your complaints. In addition, all hotels, restaurants and shops keep a книга жалоб (*kniga zhalob* – complaint book). Just asking for the book is usually enough to resolve most simple matters. On the other hand, the complaint book may also be used to inscribe your praise of an establishment's service.

C CONVERSION TABLES. For tire pressure and fluid measures—see pp. 106–107. The Soviet Union uses the metric system.

Temperature

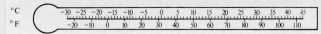

Length

Weight

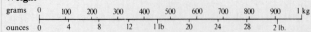

Distance

COURTESIES See also BOY MEETS GIRL. Every country has its own customs and peculiarities, and the tourist is well advised to respect them.

For instance, Muscovites are so proud of their underground (subway) system that they would take it as an insult if you were to drop a piece of paper or smoke a cigarette in the train or the station.

National pride in general is deeply rooted. Diplomacy is a virtue in any discussion.

Drinking without toasting is considered rude. If a glass is raised in your direction, return the compliment with a simple Ваше здоровье (*vashe zdorovye* – cheers!).

If you're dining in style and somebody should ask you to dance, you don't have to accept—but don't be offended. It's quite normal and even flattering to be invited to dance.

By the way, it's considered "uncultured" to enter a theatre or restaurant wearing or even carrying a hat or overcoat. Cloakrooms for leaving coats and hats are available at the entrance of all public places. A curious exception is the cinema where, in winter, overcoats are worn in the auditorium.

A simple здравствуйте (*zdrastvuytye* – "good morning" or "good day") will go a long way. Try добрый вечер (*dobriy vecher*) for "good evening". Always say до свидания (*do svidanya* – goodbye) when you leave.

How are you?	**Как поживаете?**	*kak pozhivayete*

CREDIT CARDS and TRAVELLERS' CHEQUES (кредитные карточки; дорожные чеки – *kreditniye kartochki; dorozhniye cheki*). Internationally accepted credit cards are recognized in some Soviet shops such as the art salons, as well as in Intourist hotels and hard-currency shops, but in general, the concept of the credit card—and even the personal cheque—is alien to Soviet experience.

All well-known travellers' cheques can be changed at official currency-exchange offices at the airport and in hotels. Foreign-currency shops also accept most travellers' cheques for purchases—though you're likely to be given your change in a jumble of different currencies. Remember to carry your passport and currency-control form.

Do you accept travellers' cheques?	**Вы берете дорожные чеки?**	*vi beryote dorozhniye cheki*
Can I pay with this credit card?	**Можно платить по этой кредитной карточке?**	*mozhno platit' po etoy kreditnoy kartochke*

CRIME and THEFTS (преступность; кражи – *prestupnost'; krazhi*). No social system has succeeded in eliminating crime so don't tempt fate by leaving valuables lying about or wallets jutting from hip pockets in a crowded market-place. On the bright side, however, thefts from hotel rooms are unheard of in the USSR.

Tourists should be careful not to become criminals themselves by, for instance, blackmarketeering or pocketing souvenirs.

I want to report a theft.	**Меня обокрали.**	*menya obokrali*

CURRENCY (валюта – *valyuta*). The unit of money is the rouble, divided into 100 kopeks. On price tags, rouble is abbreviated to p while kopeks are logically shortened to к; 12 p 50 is 12.50 roubles.

Coins circulate in these denominations: 1, 2, 3, 5, 10, 15, 20 and 50 kopeks, as well as 1 rouble.

Banknotes come in these denominations: 1, 3, 5, 10, 25, 50 and 100 roubles. There's no limit on how much foreign currency you may bring into the USSR. When you arrive at the border checkpoint or the airport, you'll fill out a form declaring the amount of cash and travellers' cheques you're carrying. Keep this form, for you must present it each time you change dollars or pounds into roubles. On your departure you can change your spare roubles back into foreign currency only upon presentation of the same piece of paper and supplementary receipts.

It's forbidden to import or export roubles. They're for use only within the USSR. But there's no objection to keeping a few coins as souvenirs.

Currency transactions are permitted only at banks and official currency-exchange desks at hotels, airports, etc.

CUSTOMS CONTROL (таможенный контроль – *tamozhenniy kontrol'*). See also ENTRY FORMALITIES and CURRENCY. As a general rule, all articles intended for your own use may be brought into the Soviet Union without any problem.

In addition, here are other items you can bring into the country duty-free:

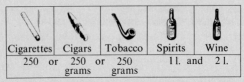

Cigarettes		Cigars		Tobacco	Spirits		Wine
250	or	250 grams	or	250 grams	1 l.	and	2 l.

You must fill out a customs declaration form to be retained until you leave the country. Be sure to declare any unusual or valuable possessions so you can take them home again without any problems. These possessions would include photographic equipment, lavish jewelry or anything else which might make any customs inspector's nose twitch. Loss of arrival customs declaration forms or incomplete listing of valuables can result in confiscation of the property in question.

Soviet customs men are particularly sensitive when it comes to reading matter. They're liable to confiscate pornography or any matter they consider to be subversive.

If you're driving, you must give customs a signed affidavit affirming that you'll drive your car out of the USSR when your tour ends.

It's illegal to sell any personal possession in the USSR.

D **DRIVING IN THE SOVIET UNION**

Planning: The paperwork involved in touring the USSR by car rules out any spontaneity. The watchword is: plan far ahead.

The first step is to consult an Intourist-approved travel agent at home at least six weeks before your trip. You'll have to submit a complete day-by-day itinerary, pay in advance for hotels or camp-sites and food, and when all reservations are confirmed, you may apply for a Soviet tourist visa.

If you're driving your own car, note that authorized entry points are limited: from Finland, Yulya and Urpala; from Poland, Brest and Shaginia; from Czechoslovakia, Uzhgorod; from Hungary, Chop; and from Rumania, Leusheny and Parubnoye. (Or you may transport your car by ship to Leningrad, Yalta, Odessa or Sochi.)

Entering the Soviet Union: To bring your car into the Soviet Union you'll need:

International Driving Licence, or your normal driving licence (with a Russian translation which may be done at the first Intourist office you encounter within the USSR)	car registration papers	Intourist accommodation and food vouchers
	nationality plate or sticker	
Motoring Tourist's Memo (confirming your itinerary)	affidavit certifying your intention to take your car out of the USSR after your tour	

The international Green Card isn't recognized. While car insurance isn't obligatory, it's wise to take out a policy with Ingosstrakh (Ингос-страх), a state insurance agency. The premium must be paid in hard currency. There are a number of branch offices in cities along tourist-approved routes.

A road tax must be paid at the border.

Regulations: Traffic regulations are complex in the Soviet Union but similar to the highway code of other countries. Drive on the right, passing on the left where prudent. The speed limit in all cities and towns is 60 kilometres per hour and 90 outside towns—except where signs permitting higher speeds are displayed. Horns may not be sounded in residential areas except to prevent an accident. In urban driving after dark, only parking lights are used. Other eccentricities: U-turns are permitted but only in designated areas usually marked separately by an arrow signal on the main traffic lights. Foreign tourists may not deviate from approved itineraries and must reach each day's destination by nightfall.

D   Use of seat belts is obligatory. Blood alcohol limit is a strictly enforced zero.

Enforcement: Traffic in cities is controlled by armed officers of the militia (police) on foot, in observation towers, patrolling on motorcycle and in radio cars. You can recognize a traffic policeman by his grey uniform and white baton.

Highways are patrolled by state traffic police on motorcycles and in yellow cars with broad blue stripes. In addition, permanent police posts are set up at key points along the roads to oversee and assist tourists. Foreign visitors must have an approved travel plan. If you don't have one, you are liable to be turned back by the police, who check all number plates.

Repairs: In the Soviet Union, as elsewhere, breakdowns are frustrating. But you'll find the locals are friendly and helpful. Not only that but every passing Russian seems to think he's a topflight mechanic and wants to prove it, particularly if your car is a rarely seen foreign model.

Unfortunately, qualified garages are few and far between in a country where the service stations can be more than 100 miles apart. And when you find one it's touch and go whether the mechanic can make repairs on the spot. If replacement parts are needed, you may as well let Intourist sign you up for a longer holiday—while you wait for the spares to arrive from abroad.

Fuel and oil: Petrol is sold in units of 10 litres and is paid for with coupons, which can be bought from Intourist. High-grade and diesel are sometimes difficult to find. On the open road it's advisable to fill up when you see a petrol station, as they are few and far between and often out of the 95-octane fuel that foreign cars take. Service stations are nearly all self-service: you pay first and then fill up.

Tire pressure			
lb./sq. in.	kg/cm^2	lb./sq. in.	kg/cm^2
10	0.7	26	1.8
12	0.8	27	1.9
15	1.1	28	2.0
18	1.3	30	2.1
20	1.4	33	2.3
21	1.5	36	2.5
23	1.6	38	2.7
24	1.7	40	2.8

Fluid measures					
litres	imp. gals.	U.S. gals.	litres	imp. gals.	U.S. gals.
5	1.1	1.3	30	6.6	7.8
10	2.2	2.6	35	7.7	9.1
15	3.3	3.9	40	8.8	10.4
20	4.4	5.2	45	9.9	11.7
25	5.5	6.5	50	11.0	13.0

Road signs: Most road signs are the standard pictographs used throughout Europe. However, you may encounter these written signs:

внимание, впереди ведутся работы	Roadworks in progress
(внимание) пешеходы	(Watch out for) pedestrians
встречное движение	Oncoming traffic
въезд запрещен	No entry
движение в один ряд	Traffic in single lane
держитесь правой стороны	Keep right
камнепад	Falling rocks
конец ограничительной зоны	End of no-passing zone
не задерживаться	No waiting
обгон запрещен	No overtaking (passing)
объезд	Diversion (detour)
ограниченная скорость	Reduce speed
одностороннее движение	One-way traffic
опасно	Danger
опасный поворот	Dangerous bend (curve)
плохая дорога	Bad road surface
светофор за сто метров	Traffic lights at 100 metres
сквозного проезда нет	No through road (dead-end road)
стоянка запрещена	No parking
сужение дороги	Bottleneck

(International) Driving Licence	**(международные) водительские права**	*(mezhdunarodniye) voditel'skiye prava*
Car registration papers	**техпаспорт автомобиля**	*tekhpasport avtomobilya*
Intourist vouchers	**талоны Интуриста**	*taloni inturista*
Motoring Tourist's Memo	**Памятка автотуриста**	*pamyatka avtoturista*

D

Export affidavit	**Письменное обяза-** **тельство о вывозе**	*pis'mennoye obyaza-* *tel'stvo o vivoze*
Are we on the right road for …?	**Мы правильно едем** **в …?**	*mi pravil'no yedem* *v*
Fill her up please, top grade.	**Полный бак,** **пожалуйста, бензин** **девяносто пятый.**	*polniy bak pozhalusta* *benzin devyanosto* *pyatiy*
Check the oil/tires/ battery.	**Проверьте масло/** **давление в шинах/** **аккумулятор.**	*prover'te maslo/* *davleniye v shinakh/* *akkumulyator*
I've had a breakdown.	**У меня авария.**	*u menya avariya*
There's been an accident.	**Произошла авария.**	*proizoshla avariya*

DRUGS. Soviet customs regulations specify that "opium, hashish and smoking utensils" may not be brought into the USSR. Since the authorities are anxious to keep the "drug culture" beyond Soviet frontiers, prohibitions are sternly enforced.

DUTY-FREE SHOPS (беспошлинные магазины – *besposhlinniye magazini*). Any convertible currency—but not roubles—may be used at Beryozka shops at airports, hotels and around town. They sell cigarettes, liquor, souvenirs and often much more at preferential prices. In addition, hard-currency shops at several different places specialize in larger items. Moscow has a furniture shop, several clothing shops and even a State Bank Gold Shop for precious stones, gold and silver. A couple of "duty-free" supermarkets stock top quality Soviet food products not widely available elsewhere, as well as luxury imported goods.

E **ELECTRIC CURRENT** (электричество – *elektrichestvo*). Mostly 220-volt, 50-cycle A.C. is used. However, 127-volt current may still be encountered in older buildings so it's wise to check. Two-pronged plugs (with thicker pins than the West European ones) are used. If you're bringing an electric razor or hair dryer with you, buy a standard continental plug adaptor, which isn't otherwise available in the USSR.

What's the voltage— 220 or 127?	**Какое напряжение** **220 или 127?**	*kakoye napryazheniye* *– dvesti dvatsat' ili* *sto dvatsat' sem'*

a battery | **батарейка** | *batareyka*

EMBASSIES (посольства – *posol'stva*)

American embassy, 19/23, Tchaikovsky St.; tel. 252-24-51/59; hours: from 9 a.m. to 1 p.m. and from 2 to 6 p.m., Monday to Friday

American consulate, 15, Petr Lavrov St., Leningrad; tel. 274-82-35; hours: from 9 a.m. to 5.30 p.m., Monday to Friday.

Australian embassy, 13, Kropotkinsky Lane; tel. 246-50-11; hours: from 8.45 a.m. to 12.30 a.m. and from 1.30 to 5 p.m., Monday to Friday

British embassy,* 14, Maurice Thorez Embankment; tel. 231-85-11; hours: from 9.30 a.m. to 12.30 p.m. and from 2.30 to 5 p.m., Monday to Friday

Canadian embassy, 23, Starokonyushenny Lane; tel. 241-91-55; hours: from 8.30 a.m. to 1 p.m. and from 2 to 5 p.m., Monday to Friday

Irish embassy, 5, Grokholski Lane; tel. 288-41-01/92; hours: from 9.30 a.m. to 1 p.m. and from 2.30 to 5.30 p.m., Monday to Friday

* also for citizens of Commonwealth countries.

Where's the British/ American embassy?	**Где английское/ американское посольство?**	*gde angliyskoye/ amerikanskoye posol'stvo*

EMERGENCIES (специальные службы – *spetsial'niye sluzhbi*). It's hard to imagine an emergency beyond the competence of Intourist or your hotel staff. Turn to your embassy or consulate in case of difficulties. However, here are some vital telephone numbers:

Fire	01
Police	02
Ambulance	03

Although we hope you'll never need them, here are a few words you might like to learn in advance:

Careful!	**Осторожно!**	*ostorozhno*
Help!	**Помогите!**	*pomogite*
Police!	**Милиция!**	*militsiya*
Stop!	**Стой!**	*stoy*
Stop thief!	**Держи вора!**	*derzhi vora*

ENTRY FORMALITIES. See also CUSTOMS CONTROLS. Before you leave home, you'll have to obtain a Soviet tourist visa to accompany your valid passport. The visa—actually a three-part leaflet (the entry

E part is ripped off on arrival), not a rubber stamp—is issued only after your accommodation inside the USSR has been confirmed by Intourist. The planning requires several weeks at the barest minimum and the help of a knowledgeable travel agent. Ordinarily, there are no vaccination or other health requirements.

At the airport or border passport control, the Soviet border guard (a soldier with a green band around his hat) will examine your documents before sending you on to the customs officials. You'll have to fill out a currency and customs declaration, listing how much money you're carrying as well as any items of potential interest to the authorities. You may have to submit to a spot check on your baggage so be sure your word of honour will stand up to closer investigation.

If an Intourist representative with a clipboard doesn't seek you out in the customs hall, proceed to the nearby Intourist office and report your arrival.

G **GUIDES and INTERPRETERS** (гид; переводчик – *gid; perevodchik*). Knowledgeable official guides are provided as part of all Intourist arrangements. For example, de luxe-class clients have the services of a guide-interpreter for up to six hours a day without extra charge. First- and tourist-class customers are entitled to guided group excursions in each city visited. If you require additional guide-interpreter services— for a private museum visit or a theatre outing—Intourist can provide it, given some advance notice.

Incidentally, don't be shy about asking all questions which come to mind, even if some may seem to be controversial. Just don't waste time with polemics or try to prove a point of view. This can be a futile and potentially mood-spoiling exercise.

We'd like an English-speaking guide.	**Нам нужен гид с английским языком.**	*nam nuzhen gid s angliyskim yazikom*
I need an English interpreter.	**Мне нужен английский переводчик.**	*mne nuzhen angliyskiy perevodchik*

H **HAIRDRESSER'S and BEAUTY SALONS** (парикмахерская; косметический кабинет – *parikmakherskaya; kosmeticheskiy kabinet*). The major hotels are the first places in which to look for barbers' shops and beauty salons.

While not obligatory, a tip won't be refused; 5 to 10 per cent would
110 be fair.

haircut	**стрижка**	*strizhka*
shampoo and set	**мытьё головы с укладкой**	*mityo golovi s ukladkoy*
permanent wave	**завивка**	*zavivka*
manicure	**маникюр**	*manikyur*
a colour chart	**окраска**	*okraska*
a colour rinse	**оттеночное полоскание**	*ottenochnoye poloskaniye*
Not too much off (here).	**(Здесь) поменьше.**	*(zdes') pomen'she*
A little more off here.	**Чуть побольше здесь.**	*chut' pobol'she zdes'*

HEALTH. In any foreign country, changes of food, climate and living habits can cause upsets. To avoid distress, take it easy on the exotic food. Do without that extra nightcap and try to squeeze some sleep into your rushed itinerary.

All the food you encounter in the cities is likely to be wholesome but it's recommendable to drink bottled mineral water rather than tap water.

If there's any medicine you think you might need, pack it before you leave home; it may be difficult to find the exact equivalent in the USSR.

HOTELS and ACCOMMODATION (гостиница – *gostinitsa*). Two organizations, Intourist and Sovincentr, operate Soviet tourist hotels. Intourist establishments may be fairly simple or more or less luxurious, while Sovincentr hotels—geared to the businessman—are all de luxe or 1st class. Incidentally, there are cheap tourist-class rooms in impressive Intourist hotels (if you're lucky) and de luxe-class rooms in mediocre hotels.

The USSR issues visas only after hotel reservations have been confirmed. All accommodation must be paid for in advance. Make bookings through a travel agency that cooperates with Intourist or Sovincentr. While of course you're free to request the hotel of your choice, the final arrangements rest with Intourist or Sovincentr who let you know the final decision on arrival at the airport.

When you arrive at your hotel, check in with the desk-clerk and hand over all your documents and vouchers. She'll return the ones she doesn't require and give you a registration form to fill in. Your passport will be kept overnight; don't forget to ask for it the next **111**

H morning. The desk-clerk won't give you the key to your room, rather a hotel pass *(propoosk)* that gives your name, length of stay and room number. You have to present this to the doorman every time you enter or leave the hotel and hand it to the attendant on your floor, the keeper of the keys. Soviet hotels employ several thousand of these *dezhurnayas* (from the French *du jour*). Mostly middle-aged women, they make tea, call taxis, take messages and so on. These women guard not only the keys but everyone's morals as well. They have the right to break down a door if they suspect hanky-panky. When you check out of the hotel, your attendant will furnish you with a pass for the doorman, proving that you have paid your bill. Intourist hotels have service desks manned by multi-lingual staff who provide information, arrange outings, make reservations and give assistance in general.

a double/single room	**номер на двоих/ на одного**	*nomer na dvoikh/na odnovo*
with bath/without bath	**с ванной/без ванны**	*s vannoy/bez vanni*
What's the rate per night?	**Какая плата за сутки?**	*kakaya plata za sutki*

I **INTERPRETERS**—see **GUIDES**

L **LANGUAGE.** Russian is understood by virtually all citizens of the Soviet Union, a multi-national society with scores of languages in daily use. Most Soviets have studied foreign languages at school but their fluency may be extremely limited. The most useful foreign languages for a visitor are English, French, German and Spanish.

The Berlitz phrase book, RUSSIAN FOR TRAVELLERS, covers all situations you're likely to encounter in your travels in the USSR and will be a welcome aid to those who are more interested in the language itself.

| Does anybody speak English? | **Говорит кто-нибудь по-английски?** | *govorit kto-nibud' po-angliyski* |

LAUNDRY and DRY-CLEANING (прачечная; химчистка – *prachechnaya; khimchistka*). The situation varies from hotel to hotel. If there's no multilingual price list in your room, ask the floor attendant.

Laundry is often done speedily by the hotel maids themselves. An express pressing service is also available. A 24-hour dry-cleaning service is available at various locations in Moscow and Leningrad.

When will it be ready?	**Когда будет готово?**	*kogda budet gotovo*
I must have this for tomorrow morning.	**Мне нужно обязательно на завтра утром.**	*mne nuzhno obyaza-tel'no na zavtra utrom*

LOST CHILDREN. Your Intourist service desk would be the first step in a hunt for a lost child (or handing over a found child). But, for the record, it would be appropriate to telephone the police to report a missing child: telephone No. 02.

A number in Moscow that deals exclusively with lost children is 294-54-92. By the way, Russians are notoriously affectionate towards children, so any wandering tyke is bound to be looked after with fervent care.

LOST AND FOUND PROPERTY (пропажи и находки – *propazhi i nakhodki*). Many are the travellers' tales of lost property turning up miraculously in Soviet hotels—occasionally even property that was meant to be discarded.

But if luck is against you, consult your Intourist service desk.

I've lost my wallet/ handbag.	**Я потерял бумажник/сумку.**	*ya poteryal bumazhnik/sumku*

MAIL (корреспонденция – *korrespondentsiya*). If you're expecting any letters or telegrams while in Moscow, don't have them addressed to you in care of a hotel. Chances are you won't know which hotel you've been assigned to until too late.

Fortunately, an efficient poste-restante (general-delivery) service operates for foreign tourists in Moscow. Have your mail addressed like this:

John Smith, Moscow K-600, USSR

To pick up your mail, go to the special K-600 poste restante (до востребования – *do vostrebovaniya*) window in the lobby of the Intourist Hotel in Gorky Street. It's open from 9 a.m. to 6 p.m. daily. You must present your passport as identification. No other document is acceptable.

M The poste-restante mailing address in Leningrad is:
C-400, Nevsky Prospekt, Leningrad, USSR.

Pick up your mail at the special C-400 window at Intourist headquarters
on Nevsky Prospekt.

Have you received any mail for me?	Есть для меня что-нибудь?	*yest' dlya menya chto-nibud'*

MAPS (планы; карты – *plani; karti*). Hotel news-stands usually
sell Moscow and Leningrad maps adequate for average tourist needs.
The Moscow Central Architectural and Planning Department issues a
large illustrated map with foreign-language legends and a comprehen-
sive indexing system. If you want a more detailed city map than those
published in this guide, you'd be wise to buy one at home like the
Leningrad and Moscow maps sold by Falk-Verlag. Stocks are frequently exhausted in the USSR. For inter-city travel, Intourist provides
simplified charts of the principal approved routes.

Note: If you're driving cross-country, don't follow your map too
literally. For security reasons, all Soviet maps contain built-in distor-
tions and inaccuracies designed to confuse potential enemies.

a street plan of...	план ...	*plan*
a road map of this region	карта дорог этого района	*karta dorog etovo rayona*

MEDICAL CARE (медицинское обслуживание – *meditsinskoye
obsluzhivaniye*). If you should fall ill, tell your Intourist guide or the
hotel service desk. A doctor will visit you in your hotel, or you may
be taken to a special clinic for tourists.

The chemist's (drugstore) is usually open from 8 a.m. to 8 or 9 p.m.
There are several all-night chemists'.

Medicine is charged to the tourist-patient but the care is free of
charge.

a doctor	доктор	*doktor*
an ambulance	скорая помощь	*skoraya pomoshch'*
hospital	больница	*bol'nitsa*
an upset stomach	расстройство желудка	*rasstroystvo zheludka*
chills	простуда	*prostuda*
a fever	жар	*zhar*

NEWSPAPERS and MAGAZINES (газеты; журналы – *gazeti; zhurnali*). If you can't decipher *Pravda* and *Izvestia,* you may fall behind on the news.

Hotel news-stands sell the newspapers of virtually all foreign Communist parties (the *Morning Star,* for instance) but a few days late. In addition, foreign tourists are allowed to buy certain non-Communist newspapers which are often available but subject to delays. However, the non-Communist papers are never displayed; you must ask for them.

For local colour, read the weekly *Moscow News.* It's also useful for theatre listings and tourist events. The pictorial magazine *Soviet Union,* issued monthly, extols the Soviet way of life.

Have you any English-language newspapers?	Есть у вас какие-нибудь английские газеты?	*yest' u vas kakiye-nibud' angliyskiye gazeti*

PETS and VETS (ветеринарная служба – *veterinarnaya sluzhba*). Until very recently, because of housing and food shortages, domestic pets were virtually unknown in the Soviet Union. However, pets are now quite common. Tourists may bring pets with them into the USSR provided they have the necessary health certificates, "issued by a competent agency of the country of origin". Such certificates must be presented to the Soviet border authorities. Veterinary service is available and quite inexpensive, although it's best to bring medicines, etc., with you.

PHOTOGRAPHY (фотография – *fotografiya*). To be certain, take all film from home. What you're accustomed to may not be available in the Soviet Union. It is not possible to have Western film processed in the USSR.

Foreigners must abide by a veritable catalogue of photographic regulations, devised for security reasons. For instance, it's forbidden to take a picture from an airplane in flight or anywhere near the Soviet border. Don't snap or sketch any object of a military character—a category embracing railway bridges, radio stations and research institutes. If the slightest doubt enters your mind, ask before you shoot.

Be prudent as well if you're tempted to photograph human-interest scenes, like consumers queueing at shops; public-spirited citizens might take offence.

May we take a picture…?	Можно снять …	*mozhno snyat'*
of this/of you	это/вас	*eto/vas*

P

I'd like a film for this camera.	Мне нужна пленка для этого аппарата.	*mne nuzhna plyonka dlya etovo apparata*
a black and white film	черно-белая пленка	*chyorno-belaya plyonka*
a colour-slide film	цветная позитивная пленка	*tsvetnaya pozitivnaya plyonka*
super-8	супер-8	*super-vosem'*
How long will it take to develop (and print) this?	Сколько нужно времени, чтобы проявить (и напечатать)?	*skol'ko nuzhno vremeni chtobi proyavit' (i na- pechatat')*

POLICE (милиция – *militsiya*). The only policemen you're likely to see are traffic patrolmen. In summer these armed officers wear grey uniforms and carry white billy clubs. In winter they bundle up in blue overcoats and fur hats.

| Where's the nearest police station? | Где ближайшее отделение милиции? | *gde blizhaysheye otdeleniye militsii* |

POST OFFICES and TELEGRAMS (почта; телеграф – *pochta; telegraf*). See also TELEPHONE. As in most European countries, the post office handles postal, telegraph and telephone services. Major hotels have their own branches of the post office, which sell stamps and accept telegrams until the evening. A round-the-clock service operates at the Central Telegraph Office (Центральный телеграф – *tsentral'niy telegraf*), 7, Gorky Street, Moscow.

In Leningrad, 24-hour-a-day service is offered at the main post office, in Soyuz Svyazi Street.

express (special delivery)	с нарочным	*s narochnim*
airmail	авиа	*avia*
registered	заказное	*zakaznoye*
poste restante (general delivery)	до востребования	*do vostrebovaniya*
A stamp for this letter/postcard, please.	Марку для этого письма/открытки, пожалуйста.	*marku dlya etovo pis'ma/otkritki pozhalusta*
I want to send a telegram to...	Я хочу послать телеграмму в...	*ya khochu poslat' telegrammu v*

PRICES (цены – *tseni*). It's impossible to compare the cost of living in the Soviet Union with other countries because of disparities in the scheme of things. For instance, subsidized housing and public transportation in the USSR are astonishingly cheap by Western ·standards but clothing and sweets are very expensive.

The following are some prices in roubles/U.S. dollars. However, they must be regarded as approximate and taken as broad guidelines.

Car rental. *Zhiguli* $15 per day, $0.16 per km., $105 per week. *Volga GAZ 24* $18 per day, $0.25 per km., $125 per week. *Moskvich 412* with chauffeur (for 10-hour day, including 240 km.), 44 roubles (excess hours 5 roubles, excess km. 20 kopeks).

Entertainment. Cinema 25–70 kopeks, theatre 0.80–3.50 roubles, Bolshoi, stall (orchestra) seat 3.50–4 roubles.

Hotels. De luxe suite 110 roubles, de luxe room 72 roubles, 1st class single 26–42 roubles, double 30–50 roubles.

Meals and drinks. Continental breakfast 2 roubles, lunch/dinner in fairly good establishment 10–25 roubles, soft drinks 50–80 kopeks, beer 1–1.50 roubles. (Prices are much higher in cooperative restaurants.)

Museums. 20–50 kopeks.

Public transport (Moscow). 5 kopeks.

Shopping at Beryozkas (see also p. 76). Caviar (1-oz. tin) 10–13 roubles, vodka (½ litre) 5–8 roubles, *matryoshka* dolls 5–100 roubles, embroidered blouses 25–50 roubles, fur hats 20–200 roubles, balalaikas 15–20 roubles.

Sightseeing. Moscow: city tour by bus 5 roubles, Kremlin 5 roubles, Moscow by river boat 3 roubles, metro stations 2 roubles, monasteries and churches 5 roubles. Leningrad: city tour by bus 4 roubles, ½-hour tour to the Hermitage 8 roubles.

Taxis. 20 kopeks at the drop of the flag, 20 kopeks per km. (30 kopeks at night).

PUBLIC HOLIDAYS (праздничные дни – *prazdnichniye dni*). With the revolution, a batch of exotic holidays were eliminated, such as the saint's day of the czarina, Coronation Day and the Festival of the Miraculous Icon of the Virgin of Kazan.

Instead, Soviet workers now take the day off for completely new holidays, such as International Women's Day and Constitution Day. Christmas is no longer officially observed although New Year's celebrations include many yuletide overtones.

P

January 1	New Year's Day
March 8	International Women's Day
May 1, 2	May Days
May 9	Victory in Europe Day
October 7	Constitution Day
November 7, 8	Revolution Days

Are you open tomorrow?	**Вы открыты завтра?**	*vi otkriti zavtra*

PUBLIC TRANSPORT. Moscow's fastest and most celebrated form of public transport, the metro (underground, or subway), carries nearly five million passengers a day in luxury. The fare is the same, regardless of the distance or the number of transfers made. Many underground stations, particularly the older ones in the city centre, are tourist attractions in themselves, remarkable for their grandiose pillars, arches, chandeliers, sculptures and mosaics.

Though less extensive and extravagant than the Moscow metro, underground transport in Leningrad is fast and dependable.

Moscow and Leningrad buses, trolley-buses and trams keep moving from about 6 a.m. to 1 a.m. The vehicles have self-service ticket dispensers. Passengers are required to drop the exact fare into a box and tear off a ticket. Defaulters are subject to the righteous indignation of the other passengers and the threat of a fine from roving ticket inspectors. It is more convenient to buy books of tickets at a newsstand.

Where's the nearest...?	**Где ближайшая ...?**	*gde blizhayshaya*
bus stop	**остановка автобуса**	*ostanovka avtobusa*
trolley-bus stop	**остановка троллейбуса**	*ostanovka trolleybusa*
tram stop	**остановка трамвая**	*ostanovka tramvaya*
metro station	**станция метро**	*stansiya metro*

R   **RADIO and TV** (радио; телевидение – *radio; televideniye*). Soviet television transmits programmes on four channels. The language problem may prove insurmountable, except for international sporting events which are always popular. All programmes are telecast in colour.

Two official radio networks broadcast to the farthest reaches of the USSR: Moscow Radio and the less solemn Radio Mayak. Radio Moscow's World Service, giving the Soviet view of international events, interspersed with Russian and Eastern European pop music, can be heard on medium wave.

If you crave news from the outer world in a language you can comprehend, the BBC and Voice of America, among other foreign stations, may be picked up at certain times of the day.

RESTAURANTS and MEAL TIMES. See also pp. 85–93. In the Soviet Union, eating houses come in all guises and price ranges. Following is a rundown of the various establishments you'll see in town and at hotels.

Bars (бар – *bar*) can be local or international, i.e. foreign currency only. The latter serve Soviet and Western spirits and are usually to be found in the major hotels. You can also order pastries and sandwiches here. For beer and appetizers, try a beer hall (пивной бар – *pivnoy bar*).

Snack bars (буфет – *bufyet*), situated in hotels, are convenient for light meals. The more modest cafeteria-style snack bars attract the local populace; on offer is a selection of hot and cold dishes rather than a full meal. There are countless subdivisions of the snack bar, usually named after the speciality they serve: those for пирожки (*pirozhki;* turnover filled with meat, cabbage or jam), for пельмени (*pyel'myeni;* kind of ravioli or meat dumpling), чай (*chay;* tea) and pastries, etc.

Restaurant (ресторан – *ryestoran*) to a Russian means a place to dance while having dinner. Some of these establishments also present floor shows.

Cafés (кафе – *kafe*), the equivalent of Western-style restaurants, provide food and drinks without the entertainment. Most close by 9 p.m., 11 at the latest.

Ice-cream parlours (кафе-мороженое – *kafe-morozhenoye*) serve drinks, mostly champagne and cocktails, as well as ice-cream.

Meal times: Lunch (обед – *obyed*) is served from about 11 a.m. to 3 p.m., dinner (ужин – *uzhin*) from 6 to 10 p.m. or so. As restaurants close at 11 p.m., Soviets usually arrive early. So if you are not eating at your hotel, it is necessary to reserve a table; ask the service bureau at your hotel to do it for you.

SHOE-SHINES (чистка обуви – *chistka obuvi*). Generally, shining shoes is a do-it-yourself affair. Your hotel room is likely to be equipped with a shoe-shine brush. And the hotel lobby may feature an electric shoe-shine machine.

S

Around Moscow there are shoe-repair stands—old-fashioned cobblers—when you may be able to get a sit-down shine.

Will you clean these shoes, please?	**Нельзя ли почистить эти туфли?**	*nel'zya li pochistit' eti tufli*

SHOPPING—AT HOME. Certain ordinary items you may take for granted at home aren't generally available in the Soviet Union, so you'd do well to pack your own—all facial tissues, for example, and your accustomed brands of toilet soap and beauty and medical aids. Experienced travellers always remember to take a rubber sink stopper of universal design to fit any plugless Soviet hotel wash-basin.

If you like chewing gum, bring your own with you (also a welcome memento for any children you may encounter).

T

TAXIS (такси– *taksi*). You can recognize a taxi by the letter *T* in a check design on the door and a green light in the top right corner of the windscreen (windshield). If the green light is on, the taxi is theoretically available, so gesticulate urgently and try to catch the driver's attention. But whether the cab driver deigns to recognize you is another question. If he does, tell him your destination (or have it written down in advance in Cyrillic letters) and see whether your luck holds—he may find it too outlandish and prefer another customer, or demand to be paid in hard currency. So, keep smiling and wait for the next taxi to come along.

However, if you can't hail one on the street go to one of the taxi ranks around town. At rush hours there are long queues but success is probable.

The telephone number for radio taxis in Moscow is 225-00-00, in Leningrad 210-00-22. You'd better have someone who speaks Russian ring for you and book a couple of hours in advance.

It does occasionally happen that, when you're waiting for a taxi, private cars draw up and offer transport. Be on your guard: fix the price in advance or you may find yourself paying a hefty fare.

TELEGRAMS—see **POST OFFICES and TELEGRAMS**

TELEPHONE (телефон – *telefon*). Local telephone calls are usually free of charge if you call from your hotel room or the service desk. You may have to dial a prefix to get an outside line.

A call from public telephone booths on the street costs 2 kopeks (2 × 1 or 1 × 2), but if you don't have them, a 10-kopek piece will do the trick. Wait for the dial tone. If there's no response or if there's a busy signal (short, anxious buzzes), replace the receiver and take your change from the coin return.

Long-distance calls may be made from your hotel or by going to the Central Telegraph Office (центральный телеграф – *tsentral'niy telegraf*), 7, Gorky Street, Moscow, or in Leningrad the telephone exchange, 3/5, Gertsena Street.

International calls are best booked through the hotel service desk, and if you are in a position to do so, well in advance. If not, arm yourself with patience; a two-hour wait is perfectly usual. Direct dialling to the West by foreigners is slowly being reintroduced. It's not possible to reverse the charges for calls from the USSR.

| Can you please get me this number? | Соедините меня, пожалуйста, с этим номером. | *soyedinite menya pozhalusta s etim nomerom* |

TIME DIFFERENCES. Moscow is three hours ahead of GMT. In summer, the clock is put one hour ahead (GMT + 4).

Los Angeles	Chicago	New York	London	**Moscow**
1 a.m.	3 a.m.	4 a.m.	9 a.m.	**noon**

The Soviet Union is so vast that it covers 11 time zones. Yet, Moscow time, also followed in Leningrad, is the standard everywhere on rail and air timetables.

TIPPING. Officially, tipping is discouraged, and you may find tips occasionally refused. But in the normal way, a gratuity for good service, given discreetly, is much appreciated (5 to 10 per cent for taxi drivers, waiters, hairdressers and barbers, 30 to 50 kopeks for porters and lavatory attendants).

TOILETS. Sign language ought to direct you to a couple of doors marked M and Ж. M is the men's room which is easy to remember. Public conveniences may also be advertised by the familiar letters, WC.

A lot of Russian plumbing is old-fashioned and clanking but operative.

| Where are the toilets? | Где туалет? | *gde tualet* |

T **TOURIST OFFICE** (туристические бюро – *turisticheskiye byuro*). You'll never be far from the helping hand of Intourist with offices at airports and hotels. For advice, tickets and complaints, the experienced linguists of Intourist are the obvious people to see.

If you have to take matters to the top, the firm's high command is located at 16, Marx Boulevard, in the heart of Moscow. The key Intourist phone number for general enquiries is 203-69-62. Intourist offices are maintained in many countries throughout the world:

British Isles: 292, Regent St., London W1; tel. 01-580 4974

Canada: 2020 University St., Montreal, Que. H3A 2A5; tel. (514) 849-6394

U.S.A.: 630 Fifth Ave. New York, NY 10020; tel. (212) 757-3884

Where's the Intourist office?	**Где бюро Интуриста?**	*gde byuro inturista*

TRAINS (поезд – *poyezd*). Although travel by air has achieved supremacy, traditional rail service remains a high Soviet priority. From the tourist's point of view it's an economical and adventurous way to see some of the countryside and meet the people. But remember to plan ahead through Intourist.

Travelling overnight, don't be surprised if the berth arrangements mix up the sexes among perfect strangers. Long-distance trains include dining-cars.

If you've no time for an excursion, drop in at a railway station anyway to look at the rolling stock and absorb the brilliant local colour.

Экспресс (*ekspress*)	Long-distance express with luxury coaches; stops only at main stations; fare is higher.
Скорый поезд (*skoriy poyezd*)	Standard long-distance train, stopping at main stations; fare is higher.
Пассажирский поезд (*pasazhirskiy poyezd*)	Inter-city train; doesn't stop at very small stations; regular fare. This type of train is seldom available for tourist travel.
Электричка (*elektrichka*)	Local train stopping at almost every station.
Международный вагон (*myezhdunarodniy vagon*)	Sleeper with individual compartments (usually double) and washing facilities

Мягкий вагон *(myakhkiy vagon)*	Sleeper with individual compartments (for two or four persons)
Купейный вагон *(kupeyniy vagon)*	Car with compartments for four persons; berths with blankets and pillows
Вагон-ресторан *(vagon restoran)*	Dining-car

When's the best train to…?	**Когда самый удобный поезд на …**	*kogda samiy udobniy poyezd na…*

TRAVELLERS' CHEQUES—see **CREDIT CARDS**

WATER (вода – *voda*). Since changes of food and water can jar delicate constitutions, it's recommended that you drink bottled mineral water, not from the tap. Soviet mineral water is always the carbonated kind.

a bottle of mineral water	**бутылка минераль-ной воды**	*butilka mineral'noy vodi*
Is this drinking water?	**Эту воду можно пить?**	*etu vodu mozhno pit'*

YOUTH HOSTELS. While there are no youth hostels per se in the USSR, Sputnik, the Soviet youth travel association, organizes group tours for students with accommodation included in the package arrangement. Unless the Sputnik holiday is planned in advance, students have to take ordinary tourist accommodation. See also page 96.

SOME USEFUL EXPRESSIONS

yes/no	**да/нет**	*da/net*
please/thank you	**пожалуйста/спасибо**	*pozhalusta/spasibo*
excuse me/you're welcome	**извините/пожалуйста**	*izvinite/pozhalusta*
where/when/how	**где/когда/как**	*gde/kogda/kak*
how long/how far	**сколько/как далеко**	*skol'ko/kak daleko*
yesterday/today/tomorrow	**вчера/сегодня/завтра**	*vchera/sevodnya/zavtra*
day/week/month/year	**день/неделя/месяц/год**	*den'/nedelya/mesyatz/god*

left/right	**левый/правый**	*leviy/praviy*
up/down	**вверх/вниз**	*vverkh/vniz*
good/bad	**хороший/плохой**	*khoroshiy/plokhoy*
big/small	**большой/маленький**	*bol'shoy/malen'kiy*
cheap/expensive	**дешевый/дорогой**	*deshoviy/dorogoy*
hot/cold	**горячий/холодный**	*goryachiy/kholodniy*
old/new	**старый/новый**	*stariy/noviy*
open/closed	**открытый/закрытый**	*otkritiy/zakritiy*
Where are the toilets?	**Где уборные?**	*gde uborniye*
Waiter!/Waitress!	**Официант!/Официантка!**	*ofitsiant/ofitsiantka*
I'd like…	**Я хотел бы…**	*ya khotel bi*
How much is that?	**Сколько это стоит?**	*skol'ko eto stoit*
What time is it?	**Который час?**	*kotoriy chas*
What does this mean?	**Что это значит?**	*chto eto znachit*

DAYS OF THE WEEK

Sunday	**воскресенье**	*voskresenye*
Monday	**понедельник**	*ponedyel'nik*
Tuesday	**вторник**	*vtornik*
Wednesday	**среда**	*sreda*
Thursday	**четверг**	*chetverg*
Friday	**пятница**	*pyatnitsa*
Saturday	**суббота**	*subbota*

MONTHS

January	**январь**	*yanvar'*
February	**февраль**	*fevral'*
March	**март**	*mart*
April	**апрель**	*aprel'*
May	**май**	*mai*
June	**июнь**	*iyun'*
July	**июль**	*iyul'*
August	**август**	*avgust*
September	**сентябрь**	*sentyabr'*
October	**октябрь**	*oktyabr'*
November	**ноябрь**	*noyabr'*
December	**декабрь**	*dekabr'*

NUMBERS

1	один	odin
2	два	dva
3	три	tri
4	четыре	chetire
5	пять	pyat'
6	шесть	shest'
7	семь	sem'
8	восемь	vosem'
9	девять	devyat'
10	десять	desyat'
11	одиннадцать	odinnatsat'
12	двенадцать	dvenatsat'
13	тринадцать	trinatsat'
14	четырнадцать	chetirnatsat'
15	пятнадцать	pyatnatsat'
16	шестнадцать	shestnatsat'
17	семнадцать	semnatsat'
18	восемнадцать	vosemnatsat'
19	девятнадцать	devyatnatsat'
20	двадцать	dvatsat'
21	двадцать один	dvatsat' odin
22	двадцать два	dvatsat' dva
30	тридцать	tritsat'
31	тридцать один	tritsat' odin
32	тридцать два	tritsat' dva
40	сорок	sorok
50	пятьдесят	pyat'desyat
60	шестьдесят	shest'desyat
70	семьдесят	sem'desyat
80	восемьдесят	vosem'desyat
90	девяносто	devyanosto
100	сто	sto
101	сто один	sto odin
102	сто два	sto dva
500	пятьсот	pyatsot
1,000	тысяча	tisyacha

Index

An asterisk (*) next to a page number indicates a map reference. Where there is more than one set of page references, the one in bold type refers to the main entry.